Northumbria Walks with Children

Stephen Rickerby

Copyright © Stephen Rickerby, 1998

Reprinted 2001

All Rights Reserved. No part of this publication may be reproduced, stored in a retrieval system, or transmitted in any form or by any means – electronic, mechanical, photocopying, recording, or otherwise – without prior written permission from the publisher.

Published by Sigma Leisure – an imprint of
Sigma Press, 1 South Oak Lane, Wilmslow, Cheshire SK9 6AR, England.

British Library Cataloguing in Publication Data
A CIP record for this book is available from the British Library.

ISBN: 1-85058-619-5

Typesetting and Design by: Sigma Press, Wilmslow, Cheshire.

Cover photograph: Low Force, Teesdale

Maps and photographs: Jeremy Semmens

Printed by: MFP Design & Print

PREFACE

Northumbria stretches from the Tees, north to the Scottish border, including both Northumberland and Durham. There is a rich variety of landscapes in which to walk with children – a variety which the walks chosen for this book try to reflect. Scenery ranges from the dune-fringed coast of North Northumberland as at Seahouses (Walk 2) and Bamburgh (Walk 8) to riverbank rambles inland as at Allen Banks (Walk 11) and Cotherstone, in Teesdale (Walk 21).

The North-East is, of course, equally rich in history and in industrial heritage. Walks in this book will allow you and your children to sample this inheritance across two millennia: from the Roman remains of Hadrian's Wall (Walk 10), through the monastic relics of Holy Island and Durham (Walks 7 and 15) to the legacy of the Industrial Revolution as at Causey Arch (the world's oldest surviving railway bridge, Walk 13) and Westgate in Weardale (Walk 15).

Particular sites such as waterfalls like High and Low Force on the Tees (Walks 18 and 19) and castles and cathedrals like Dunstanburgh, Warkworth and Durham (Walks 3, 4 and 15) are also featured. Other child-friendly attractions include the steam railways at Etal (Walk 1) and the Tanfield Railway at Causey Arch. Sandy beaches add to the appeal of the walks at Seahouses, Bamburgh and Tynemouth (Walk 9), as well as being easily accessed from several other routes, including the glorious Embleton Bay from the Craster and Dunstanburgh route.

Walking with children necessitates a degree of forward planning and the walks are introduced with vital information such as the location of toilets and refreshments, how accessible a route is likely to be with a pushchair and what the terrain is like. This is intended to assist your planning, but you, of course, will still need to assess the aptitude of your children to undertake a particular route, at a particular season and in particular weather conditions.

All the walks have been chosen because they are potentially interesting experiences for children and are not too demanding. They are meant for children to walk with adult guidance: paths can be slippery and roads have traffic even in the hills. The majority include sections of cross-country walking, which require strong and sensible footwear for the pedestrian, if not the child in a backpack. Sensible protection against the weather – rain or shine - is also a factor on a walk that may take a small child a mile or more from the nearest road or shop.

Maps are suggested for each walk. The Ordnance Survey Pathfinder and Leisure Maps are the best, and these are widely available in bookshops. Pathfinder maps are to be replaced by a new series of Explorer maps by 2002. In Northumbria, the Ordnance Survey plans to replace Pathfinders by Explorers by 2001.

The checklists of things for children to look out for along the walk are all based on what we have actually seen. Some sights are inevitably seasonal, and some you may just miss. So, set a target of seeing six or seven, rather than all ten, to avoid disappointment.

Older, more confident children may be more actively involved if allowed to go ahead a little to find the way. A further useful motivational tip may be to describe your activity as exploring - avoiding the 'w'-word altogether. Painting the experience as adventure and investigation may well be a sound marketing strategy with many children.

Starting and finishing points are intended to offer somewhere to go before, or more likely after, the walk. In towns and larger villages there will be plenty of shops and refreshments, as well as other attractions, but some more rural beginnings such as at Allen Banks or Holwick, may only offer a picnic site or single pub. Suggestions are made for nearby places to drive on to – always in a matter of minutes.

To make the book easy to use, you'll find different styles of text:

Plain text, just like this, to give directions for the adults.

☺ Text with a smiley face indicates interesting features of the walk for children.

Q The same typestyle is used for quiz questions. These are intended to stimulate discussion along the way. Be sure to hide the answers!

Smaller, script-style, text is used for background information. This should provide some back-up for fielding penetrating questions.

Enjoy your walks with children in Northumbria!

Acknowledgements

My thanks go, as always, to my wife Debbie and daughter Katie for helping me on the walks.

Stephen Rickerby

CONTENTS

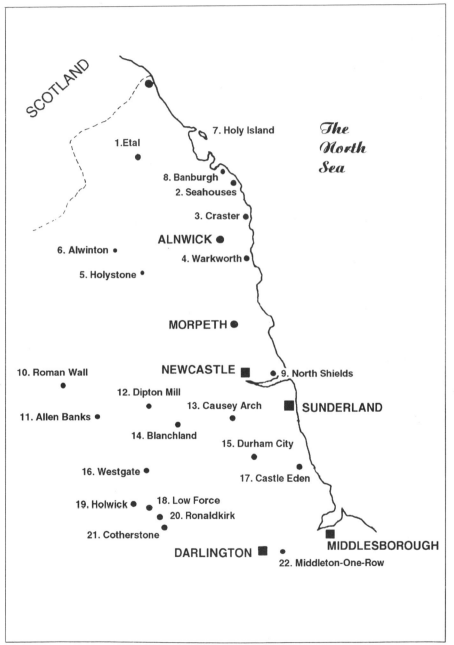

SCOTLAND

7. Holy Island

The North Sea

1.Etal

8. Banburgh

2. Seahouses

3. Craster

ALNWICK ●

6. Alwinton ●

4. Warkworth ●

5. Holystone ●

MORPETH ●

NEWCASTLE ■

10. Roman Wall

● 9. North Shields

12. Dipton Mill

13. Causey Arch

SUNDERLAND ■

11. Allen Banks ●

14. Blanchland

15. Durham City

16. Westgate ●

17. Castle Eden

19. Holwick ●

18. Low Force

20. Ronaldkirk

21. Cotherstone

MIDDLESBOROUGH ■

DARLINGTON ■

22. Middleton-One-Row

Location map (numbers refer to walks)

New "Explorer" Maps from the Ordnance Survey

The Ordnance Survey has a programme of introducing 'Explorer' maps, which replace the 1:25 000 Pathfinder maps suggested for many of the walks in this book. At the time of writing, three Explorer maps have been published for parts of Northumbria, two of which are suitable for the following walks:

Walk no	Walk	Explorer Maps
2	Seahouses	340 Holy Island and Bamburgh
7	Holy Island	340 Holy Island and Bamburgh
8	Bamburgh	340 Holy Island and Bamburgh
9	North Shields & Tynemouth	316 Newcastle upon Tyne

There has been some expansion of Outdoor Leisure map coverage since the book was first published. Alternatives to Pathfinder maps are as follows:

Walk no	Walk	O.S.Outdoor Leisure Maps
5	Holystone	Outdoor Leisure 16 - The Cheviot Hills
6	Alwinton	Outdoor Leisure 16 - The Cheviot Hills
10	Roman Wall	Outdoor Leisure 43 - Hadrian's Wall
11	Allen Banks	Outdoor Leisure 43 - Hadrian's Wall
12	Dipton Mill	Outdoor Leisure 43 - Hadrian's Wall
14	Blanchland	Outdoor Leisure 43 - Hadrian's Wall

Walks 18, 19, 20 and 21 are still on Outdoor Leisure 31, but this has been re-named 'Teesdale and Weardale'.

1. ETAL

Etal is a chocolate-box village of idyllic cottages, some thatched, stretched along its single street, from the manor to the ruined castle. Etal, pronounced 'e-etle' (as in 'beetle') is the most northerly village in this book – and the closest to Scotland, which, as the crow flies, is only 4 miles to the west. The gardens of the manor are open to the public only on advertised fund-raising days.

Etal Castle ruins and museum and the steam railway to Heatherslaw are the principal diversions for children. The castle is open from Easter to October. Its museum includes an exhibition telling the story of the Battle of Flodden (1513). The entrance is through the car park and round the back of the building which houses the exhibition – signposted to the railway. The railway has a halt at Etal from which you can catch the little train to Heatherslaw.

Starting Point:	Etal Castle car park (Grid ref. NT 925394)
Distance:	2½ miles
Terrain:	Apart from the village itself, and some of the return along metalled lane, the terrain is mostly unsurfaced field and woodland paths. There are no especially steep slopes.
Maps:	OS Pathfinder 451 Norham and 463 Coldstream
Public Toilets:	Etal Castle car park
Refreshments:	The post office in Etal has a small tearoom. Alternatively, there is the Black Bull, Etal or, if you take the steam train ride, Heatherslaw Corn Mill café.
Pushchairs:	The sections around the village, down as far as the river and up to the manor are suitable for pushchairs.

☞ You should pass most of these. See how many you can spot:
- ☐ a sycamore, a beech and an ash tree
- ☐ a thatched pub
- ☐ two cannon
- ☐ a ford
- ☐ rosehips or a blackberry bush
- ☐ someone fishing
- ☐ a ruin, apart from the castle
- ☐ ducks
- ☐ hawthorn or elder trees
- ☐ a pheasant

Etal castle

1. Start from the car park next to the castle. Walk up the drive towards the main street, but turn left when you reach the end of the drive and walk, as signposted, towards the river.

☺ The castle was built in the 14th century – over 600 years ago.

Q: What is the name of the river we are going to walk to now?
A: River Till (on the waymark post at the end of the castle drive).

2. Walk down the lane to the river's edge, where there is a ford. However, you should not cross this. Instead, turn right and walk along to the end of the old footbridge. Do not cross this either! Turn right again and walk up the short flight of steps to join the footpath, heading left, parallel to the River Till. Keep going along the riverbank.

3. Reaching some ruins adjacent to a weir on your left, you will find yourself joining a wider track.

☺ We are now at Barleymill Bank. In the past, the weir in the river would help build up speed in the river to drive the mill's waterwheel.

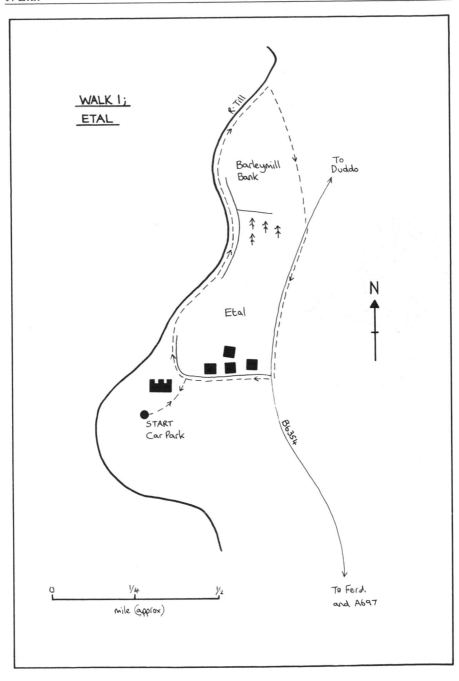

WALK 1;
ETAL

R. Till

Barleymill
Bank

To
Duddo

Etal

N

START
Car Park

B6354

0   ¼   ½
mile (approx)

To Ford.
and A697

4. Bear left along this track to reach a stile and gate combination. Negotiate these and continue along the path, passing by another footbridge. Keep going, through the trees, until you approach a leftward sweep of the river.

☺ Keep your eyes peeled now. We are looking for a large horse chestnut (conker) tree on our right. Next to it there should be a conifer, with a path between the two.

5. Turn right on to the path between the two trees. Walk up behind the horse chestnut to cross a waymarked stile.

You will need to look carefully. If you have actually begun to follow the river leftward you have gone too far. At the same time, avoid being tempted by an earlier gully next to a narrow tributary and two tiny wood-fenced enclosures. The waymarking on the stile will confirm you are on course.

6. Walk up the gully beyond the stile and bear right at its end. Opposite you should see a conifer plantation and, as you scan left, a clutch of three and then two deciduous trees. In the gap is waymarked gate. Make for this target, and then, on the other side, follow the path straight ahead across the pasture.

☺ The hills we can see over to the right are the Cheviots. These hills are quite distinctive because of their rounded shape. This is because they are made of rock which is volcanic in origin.

The Cheviot Hills form the setting for Walk 6 (Alwinton) and are visible from several of the walks in north Northumberland.

7. The path ends at a stile. Cross it and walk to the right alongside the metalled road to return to Etal — at the opposite end of the village from the castle.

On the approach to the village, there is a brown tourist information sign.

Q: What do all these symbols tell us about Etal and its surroundings?

A: There are gardens, somewhere to eat and a castle in Etal, a museum and blacksmith in Ford, as well as a steam railway and somewhere else to eat.

As you walk along there are views over to the Till on your right, and you may be able to point out buildings you past on the early part of the walk.

8. Turn right and walk along the village street to the castle car park.

Other Places of Interest in the Area

Heatherslaw and Etal Light Railway

This light steam railway has open carriages, so be prepared for the elements. An hourly service operates from March until October, from mid-morning until late afternoon. There are Santa specials in December. For details telephone the Heatherslaw Light Railway Company on (01890) 820444 or 820317. At Heatherslaw, you will find child-friendly service at the Corn Mill's Granary TeaRooms, including high chairs and toys. If you prefer to drive rather than catch the train, it is about a mile and a half in the direction of Ford, and is signposted.

The Corn Mill itself has been restored to grind locally grown wheat using water power, as it did in the 19th century. There are tours available, with demonstrations and fresh Heatherslaw bread to buy from the shop. The mill is open from around Easter until the end of October (tel. 01890 820 338).

Ford

Ford is 3 miles from Etal, and is well signposted. Lady Waterford Hall was originally the village school. It houses murals painted by Louisa, Marchioness Waterford, over a period of 21 years, depicting the children of the village in a series of Bible stories. It is open in the morning and again in the afternoon, daily, from March to October (tel. 01890 820524).

Errol Hut Smithy

This is a working, traditional, country smithy, welcoming visitors and specialising in wrought iron. There is also a woodwork shop. Open daily from 10am to 5pm (tel. 01890 820317). Errol Hut Smithy is at Letham Hill and is signposted from Etal (turn right out of the village and then left).

2. SEAHOUSES

Seahouses lies on the Northumberland coast and is well signposted from the A1 at Alnwick. Originally a fishing village, the settlement has developed a tourism-based economy over the last 25 years or so. Fishing itself is now much curtailed and the harbour not as busy as it was. Nevertheless, there are boats to be seen all year and the summer season brings a marked increase in activity.

To the north of the village St Aidan's Dunes stretch all the way to Bamburgh. The beaches are of beautiful fine sand – there are none better on a hot summer's day. Coupled with the offshore scenery of the rocky Farnes, they set a spectacular scene all year round. The walk itself begins along the beach. Tide times can be checked with Seahouses Tourist Information Office on 01665 720885. After a turn around the harbour, the full route takes you through the two villages of Seahouses and North Sunderland before returning to the dunes across fields.

Starting Point:	Monks House (Grid ref. NU 204336)
Distance:	4 miles
Terrain:	Sand dunes and beach followed by metalled street and then unsurfaced field path.
Map:	OS Pathfinder 465 Belford, Seahouses and Farne Islands
Public Toilets:	Seahouses (car park)
Refreshments:	Seahouses and North Sunderland
Pushchairs:	Much of the route is suitable – certainly the streets of Seahouses and North Sunderland, plus the harbour side and the links from Seahouses to North Sunderland.

☞ You should pass most of these. See how many you can spot:

☐   spiky marram grass
☐   shells
☐   seaweed
☐   a horse-rider
☐   a lifebelt
☐   a kite or a sandcastle
☐   North Sunderland lifeboat station
☐   seagulls
☐   a weather vane on a church
☐   black and brown cattle

The harbour, Seahouses

1. Start from the dunes to the south of Monks House. Walk across the dunes, using one of the pathways, to the beach and turn right along it.

Monks House is a stone-built house on your right as you drive north from Seahouses to Bamburgh. Along the roadside are parking places, and your exact starting point is going to depend upon how close to Monks House you are able to park. Ease of parking varies considerably with the season. If you are able to park very close to Monks House then use the waymarked bridleway beside the garden to access the beach; if not, then there are a number of paths available at intervals through gaps between the dunes.

☺ The island we can see is one of the Farnes. These islands are a bird sanctuary now, but in the past were used by hermits, including St Cuthbert.

There are boat trips to and around the Farnes from Seahouses harbour, which you will reach later on the walk.

2. Walk along the beach until, at the end, you ascend a flight of steps up to the links. Turn left and walk along the top of the seabanks into Seahouses.

☺ Seahouses gets it name because that is what it was originally – houses by the sea. Later we will walk through the village of North Sunderland, which Seahouses grew from. In the past there was only a small fishing community around the harbour, but tourism has led Seahouses to expand into a small seaside resort.

3. On entering Seahouses, take the first road left, just in front of the Viking Restaurant, and walk down to the harbour – as signposted.

☺ Look at the boats in the harbour. They have registration numbers – similar to cars. Local boats are all BK numbers – BK is for Berwick (upon Tweed), which is the local coastal town. Seahouses is only a village and so does not qualify for its own letters.

Taking appropriate care, children will probably want to explore the harbour and its piers. Make the Harbour Office your rendezvous point – it is a wooden hut below the imposing Bamburgh Castle Hotel, on your right when you first arrive at the harbour side.

4. From the Harbour Office, walk up the steps away from the harbour and along the street between the Olde Ship and the Bamburgh Castle Hotel.

The Seahouses Marine Life and Fishing Heritage Centre (tel. 01665 721257 or 720712) is along here. You may wish to visit it (between Easter and October) to see something of Seahouses past.

5. Then continue straight ahead along the length of the main street and, at the road junction, straight ahead again into North Sunderland.

Escape Route: Turn right on to the footpath and emerge at the end of the car park. Walk though this, past the Tourist Information Centre, and turn left to return to the dunes.

Q: To which saint is the parish church dedicated?
A: St Paul (look at the sign in the churchyard on your left).

6. Carry on through North Sunderland to the post office. Turn right at the road junction and walk past the Longstone House Hotel.

Especially in summer, the ice creams at the post office or tables outside the Longstone may be welcome refreshment pauses.

7. Walk along the lane beyond the Longstone House Hotel.

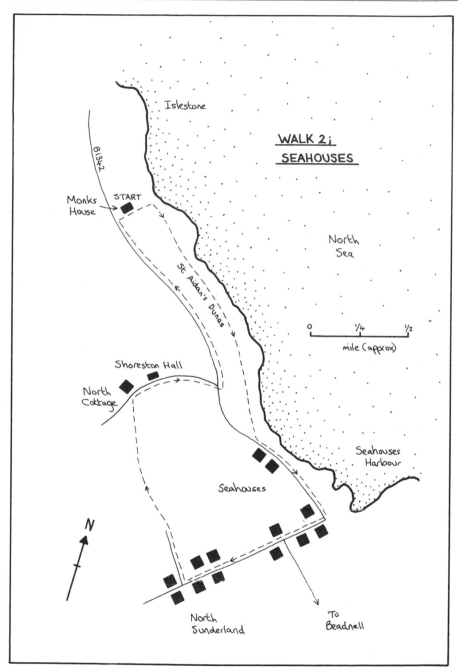

Islestone

WALK 2;
SEAHOUSES

B1342

Monks
House

START

North
Sea

St Aidan's Dunes

0   ¼   ½
mile (approx)

Shoreston Hall

North
Cottage

Seahouses
Harbour

Seahouses

N

North
Sunderland

To
Beadnell

☺ The castle we can see over to the left is Bamburgh Castle. In Bamburgh there is a museum to commemorate Grace Darling, who set off in a rowing boat – from the Longstone lighthouse on the Farnes – in 1838 to rescue, with the help of her father, nine shipwrecked sailors from the Forfarshire. She became an instant national heroine.

8. Beyond the end of speed limit signs, turn left over a stone stile, on to the signposted public footpath towards Shoreston Hall.

Q: How far is it to Shoreston Hall?

A: Three-quarters of a mile (on the signpost).

Escape Route: Instead of crossing the stile, continue straight down the lane to the dunes.

9. Cross the pasture, bearing slightly right and making for the field corner. From there continue in the same direction to the brow of the rise in the field and look for a gate in the left-hand corner ahead. Make for that gate. Continue across two more pasture fields to reach the metalled lane.

Q: What is the name of the cottage with the sundial?

A: North Cottage.

10. Turn right alongside the metalled lane and walk on as far as the T-junction with the coastal road. Turn left to return to Monks House.

Other Places of Interest in the Area

The Farne Islands

These rocky islands, formed of resistant Whin Sill, lie just offshore. Inner Farne is clearly visible from the beach. A seabird sanctuary and grey seal breeding ground, the islands may be visited by boat from Seahouses harbour.

Bamburgh

Bamburgh is an attractive, green village 3 miles to the north of Seahouses, nestling in the shelter of its imposing castle. A fortification has stood on this promontory since the 6th century and Bamburgh was, in pre-conquest days, the capital of the ancient kingdom of Bernicia – the forerunner of

Northumbria. The castle is open to the public daily from April to October
(tel. 01668 214515)|.

Holy Island (Lindisfarne)

Still further to the north is the island of Lindisfarne, its castle and ruined
7th-century monastery. Connected to the mainland by causeway, it is accessible only at low tide and you will need to check the times before setting
out. Tourist Information Centres such as the one at Seahouses can help.
The Museum of Island Life is open between Easter and October; it recreates
the way of life of a fishing family living and working from 18th-century
Hillcroft Cottage. The museum is a sister enterprise of the Seahouses Marine Life Museum, and further information may be obtained from there.

3. CRASTER AND DUNSTANBURGH CASTLE

The Northumberland fishing village of Craster lies 6 miles to the east of the A1. From Alnwick follow signposts to Seahouses initially, and then to Craster and Dunstanburgh Castle.

The ruined castle of Dunstanburgh is set dramatically on the rocky shore just over a mile from the village and can be reached only on foot. The ruins at Dunstanburgh are managed by English Heritage and are open to the public (tel. 01665 576231). There is a charge.

This walk will allow you to explore the village and harbour at Craster before wandering along the shore to the ruins, returning across the fields.

Starting Point:	Craster Tourist Information Office (Grid ref. NU 246198)
Distance:	3 miles
Terrain:	Mostly on unsurfaced paths, muddy after wet weather, adjacent to the rocky shore, and then over pastureland and finally, briefly, through woodland.
Map:	OS Pathfinder 477 Embleton and Alnmouth
Public Toilets:	Craster Tourist Information Office, including nappy changing facility.
Refreshments:	Craster has a couple of cafés and a pub (the Jolly Fisherman) which has a panoramic harbour view.
Pushchairs:	The village itself is suitable, as is the walk to the castle in dry summer weather, though not the return loop over the fields.

☞ You should pass most of these. See how many you can spot:

- ☐ an English Heritage symbol
- ☐ a tree house
- ☐ a fishing boat
- ☐ a crab or lobster pot
- ☐ a lifebelt
- ☐ a crab
- ☐ a ruined castle
- ☐ a view of some sand dunes
- ☐ gorse
- ☐ a National Trust symbol

Dunstanburgh castle

Around the Tourist Information Office and its car park, there are a number of displays about the local heritage. You may think it is a good idea to encourage the children to look at these before setting out.

☺ Craster used to be more than just a fishing village. There used to be fish and 'chips'! See if you can find out what the chips were.

The chips were pieces of ground Whinstone which was quarried here for use as roadstone.

☺ The Whin chips were taken down to the harbour and loaded on ships there. When we reach the harbour we will be able to see the remains of the loading gear.

Adjacent to the car park is the Arnold Memorial Nature Reserve – one of 60 run by the Northumberland Wildlife Trust. You may want to explore this (admission is free) on your return from the walk.

1. Start from the Tourist Information Office car park by turning right alongside the metalled lane into Craster village.

2. At the harbour, turn left along Dunstanburgh Road.

Children will probably want to explore the harbour. The quays are accessible and the left-hand one has a plaque about the building of the harbour. At the end of the other is a squarish arch. This was the base for the loading gear used to pour the Whin chips into the holds of coasters.

Q: When was the harbour built?

A: 1906 (on the plaque).

3. Pass through the gate and follow the main coastal path all the way to the castle gates.

☺ Dunstanburgh Castle was built over 600 years ago. During the Wars of the Roses it was a Lancastrian (red rose) stronghold, eventually overrun by the white rose Yorkists.

As you climb the castle mound you will be able to see the glorious sandy beach and dunes of Embleton Bay beyond. To visit this, follow the path to the left of the mound or drive to Embleton after you have finished the walk.

4. From the castle, head back down to the fenced fields. Go through the first gate and then head diagonally up to the right.

The right of way shown on the OS map would have you walk as far as the next fence and then turn a right angle to climb the slope. However, it is clear on the ground that the diagonal route is the one people use and it does bring you to a stile. This is all National Trust land.

5. Cross the stile at the top and walk along the track until it dips down. At the bottom, turn left through a kissing gate and walk along the base of the cliffs on your left.

☺ These cliffs are as rugged as they are because of the quarrying which went on in Crater until the 1930s. This particular stretch is called Dunstanburgh Heughs. 'Heugh' is a local dialect word for rocky hill.

6. The path will bring you to a waymarked gate. Pass through it, and walk through the woods to return to the car park.

Before you cross the road, have the children look at the sign at the end of the woodland path.

Q: Who owns Dunstanburgh Heughs?

A: The National Trust.

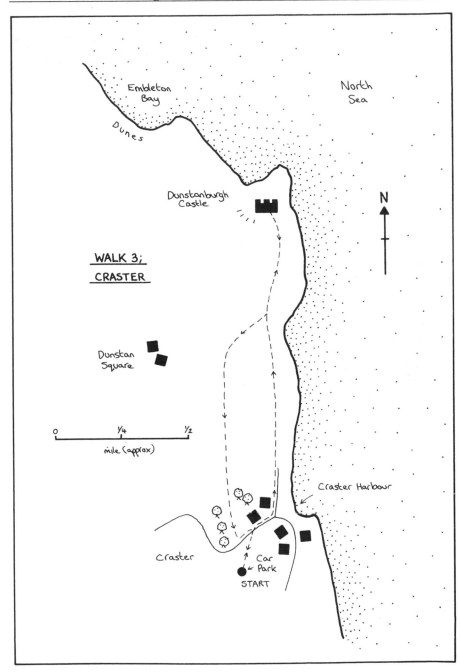

The National Trust is a charity. It raises money to look after historic buildings (like Dunstanburgh Castle) and parts of the countryside like Dunstanburgh Heughs so that they can be kept for people to enjoy.

Other Places of Interest in the Area

Alnwick

The market town of Alnwick is 7 miles to the west. Market day is Saturday. Alnwick Castle (tel. 01665 510777) is the seat of the Dukes of Northumberland and houses collections of paintings, porcelain and furniture. The castle is open from Easter to September, but not on Fridays. In June there is the week-long Alnwick Fair – a costumed re-enactment of the medieval fair. Alnwick Tourist Information Office's telephone number is 01665 510665.

Seahouses

Seahouses (see Walk 2) is a larger and more commercialised harbour village to the north of Craster. There are amusement arcades there and boat trips are run to the Farne Islands. In addition there is the Marine Life and Fishing Heritage Centre (tel. 01665 721257 or 720712), which is open from Easter to October.

Howick Hall

Howick Hall is just south of Craster and can be reached by car by heading out of Craster village, initially in the direction of Alnwick. After passing through the stone gate, turn left at the crossroads and drive on for 2 miles. The extensive gardens here are the main attraction since the house itself is not open to the public. The grounds, both formal and natural, are open in the summer months – telephone 01665 577285.

4. WARKWORTH

The small, historic town of Warkworth is virtually enclosed by a meander of the River Coquet. It consists essentially of a single 'bailey' street, which runs down from the castle at the top to the square at the bottom. Warkworth Castle is a prominent baronial fortification of 12th-century vintage, and home to the aristocratic Percy family until the 16th century.

Beginning from the market square, the walk takes you along the pretty banks of the Coquet, returning across fields to the castle itself and back to the market square via a narrow, medieval lane. It is an easy route, rich in history.

Starting Point:	Warkworth market cross (Grid ref. NU 246061)
Distance:	2¼ miles
Terrain:	Riverside and field paths
Map:	OS Pathfinder 501 Amble and Lynemouth
Public Toilets:	Warkworth, Hotspur Lane
Refreshments:	Cafés and pubs in Warkworth
Pushchairs:	Suitable throughout

☞ You should pass most of these. See how many you can spot:

☐ a market cross

☐ the time on a church clock

☐ a spire

☐ swans

☐ a weir

☐ a flag

☐ a boat landing

☐ a horsebox

Warkworth castle

1. Start from the market cross with the Masons Arms behind you. Head
left, alongside the road, towards the Coquet, passing the Black Bull
Hotel on your left.

*Approaching the Coquet, there is a stone arch leading through to the old,
stone packhorse bridge. Inside the arch is a plaque. Maybe the children can go
into the arch to read this.*

Q: When was the bridge built?

A: The 14th century

☺ This narrow, old bridge carried all the traffic in and out of Warkworth for
over 600 years – until 1965 when the modern road bridge was opened.
The river here is called the Coquet.

2. Before reaching the old stone arch, turn left to follow the riverside
path, signposted Mill Walk. Keep going until you reach a waymark
sign at the end of Hotspur Lane.

Escape route: Turn left along Hotspur Lane to return to the town
centre.

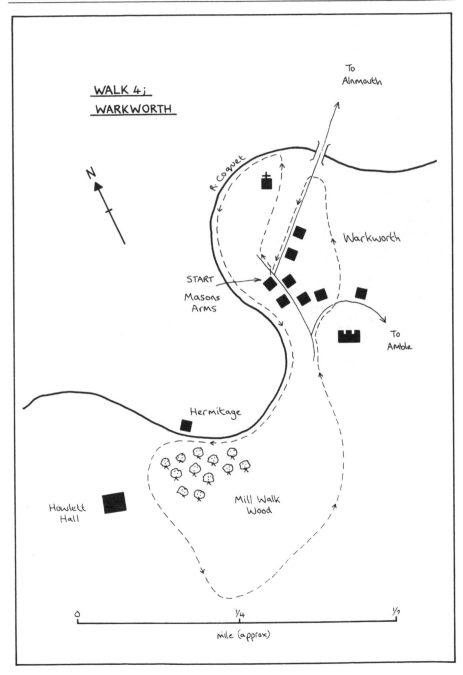

WALK 4;
WARKWORTH

To Alnmouth

N

R. Coquet

Warkworth

START
Masons
Arms

To Amble

Hermitage

Mill Walk
Wood

Howlett
Hall

0   ¼   ½

mile (approx)

3.   Walk straight ahead along the now unsurfaced riverside path of Mill Walk in the direction of Howlet Hall.

Q: How far is it to Howlet Hall?

A: ¾ mile

☺ We will pass Howlet Hall on the way to the castle.

Walking round this river bend or meander we can see how the outer bank is steeper than the inner. This is because the river current has greater force there and can wear the bank away to form what is called a river cliff. On the inside of the bend is a muddy beach, deposited by the slower current. This is called a slip off slope.

There are plenty of seats along this stretch. As you round the meander look behind for an excellent photo opportunity of the castle ramparts towering above the Coquet.

☺ Warkworth Castle was built 800 years ago. It was home to the Percy family – the Dukes of Northumberland.

4.   When you reach a public footpath signposted to Warkworth Castle on your left, ignore it and carry straight on.

Escape route: Take the path up to the castle and return to the market square from there.

5.   On reaching a single wooden gate, pass straight through. Keep walking by the riverside until you reach a point opposite Warkworth Hermitage.

In summer (from Easter to September) you can take the rowing boat ferry over the Coquet to visit this English Heritage site.

☺ A hermit is someone who deliberately lives all alone – cut off from other people. This is often for religious reasons. A chapel was hewn from the rock here 600 years ago. The last hermit was George Lancaster, who lived here in the 16th century.

6.   Turn left up the surfaced lane, away from the river. Keep going until you reach the stone cottage, which is Howlet Hall, at the top of the rise. Pass through the gate and bear left at the T-junction of lanes. Keep going until you come to Crossroads Cottage.

☺ Look into the garden of the cottage. The shelter is a boat!

7. Opposite Crossroads Cottage is a signposted public footpath lead-ing to Warkworth Castle. Turn left along this field-edge path.

☺ Look ahead and we can see the castle!

8. Another path joins the route from the right. Carry on, bearing slightly left along the field edge towards the ruins and a wooden gate. Follow the path beyond, across the pasture, bearing slightly left again, and continue in similar fashion until you access the grounds of the castle itself.

☺ When we near the castle, look down to the river and see if you can spot the path we walked along earlier.

Ignore a path on your left which leads back down to the river. The public right of way is through the grounds of the castle. To visit the castle, head right to the bridge over the moat. It is open weekends, from Easter to September.

9. To continue the walk, follow the path to the left of the castle, de-scending stone steps into the moat.

☺ Castles were often surrounded by moats filled with water to make them more difficult to attack. Drawbridges were used to let people in and out when there was no danger.

10. Follow the path until you emerge from the grounds at the top of the main street.

Escape route: Simply walk down to the market square.

11. Turn right along Castle Terrace, crossing the street when it is safe.

This road can be busy. Children running ahead through the castle grounds may need to be warned not to cross the road.

12. At the end of Castle Terrace is number 5, which has a Shakespeare door knocker. Turn left, hard by the side of the house, and follow the dogleg path right then left. Follow the long vennel (narrow pathway) down to its end.

☺ This back lane is parallel to the main street of Warkworth. To either side are the long and narrow gardens of the houses. The lane has been here for hundreds of years – since the Middle Ages at least.

13. At the end of the narrow lane, turn left to the river end of the main street. Turn left up the street to return to the market square.

Other Places of Interest in the Area

Amble Marina and Braid

There is a picnic site at this small seaport built at the Coquet's mouth.

The Northumberland Coastal Route

This is a well signposted drive along the spectacular and often dune-fringed Northumberland coastline, taking in Alnmouth, Seahouses and Bamburgh en route.

Alnmouth

The seaside village of Alnmouth has a sandy beach. There are cafés and pubs along its single street.

5. HOLYSTONE

The pretty little village of Holystone lies in Upper Coquetdale. It is signposted from the minor road that leads up the dale from the market town of Rothbury towards Harbottle and Alwinton. It would be possible to combine this walk with that from Alwinton (Walk 6). The Rose and Thistle in Alwinton or Salmon Inn here in Holystone would be good pub lunch stops if you decide to make a day of it.

The Lady's Well beauty spot in Holystone is a tranquil, walled pool with a Celtic stone cross at its centre. Set in a garden, the well still provides water for the village and takes its name from the Augustinian priory of St Mary the Virgin, established here in the 12th century and home to a community of canonesses.

The walk begins on the edge of Holystone Forest, and takes in the Lady's Well on a circular route across the fields via the hamlet of Sharperton.

Starting Point:	Holystone Forest Walks car park (Grid ref. NT 951026) – signposted from the village.
Distance:	2¾ miles
Terrain:	A mixture of lanes and field paths, some of which can be muddy. There is a short initial stretch through the forest.
Map:	OS Pathfinder 499 Harbottle or Outdoor Leisure map 16 The Cheviot Hills
Toilets:	The Salmon Inn (for customers)
Refreshments:	The Salmon Inn
Pushchairs:	The lanes around the village, including one to the Lady's Well, are more suitable than the actual route described.

☞ You should pass most of these. See how many you can spot:

- ☐ a fire beater
- ☐ an oak leaf
- ☐ moss
- ☐ a Celtic cross
- ☐ an animals' drinking trough
- ☐ a molehill
- ☐ a tractor
- ☐ an animal feed hopper
- ☐ a delivery box in a bus shelter
- ☐ a beehive

The Forest Walks' car park is signposted from Holystone village. There are picnic tables set among the trees. Waymarked walks have been laid out through the forest, and you could follow one of these as an alternative to this route.

1. Start from the Forest Walks' display board. Facing it, head right, away from the road, to a gate. Pass through.

☺ To start this walk, we are following the green symbols – so keep an eye out for them.

2. At the second waymark post, turn right towards the Lady's Well. Walk along the forest path until you come to a kissing gate. Pass through and walk along the field-edge path.

☺ On the right here are long mounds which may well be the remains of medieval farming strips. In a typical Middle Ages village, the peasants who lived there would each have strips of land to work – to grow their crops. They would have some well-drained, fertile strips and some which were not so productive, or heavy and damp. This was to try to give everyone a fair share.

3. Following the waymark arrows, bear slightly right until you reach a farm gate. Turn left to the lych gate which gives you access to the Lady's Well.

☺ This square pool is still a well for the village. It is called the Lady's Well because Holystone used to have a community of canonesses (nuns) whose priory was dedicated to St Mary (our Lady as they would have called her). The cross in the centre is called a Celtic cross. It has a slightly different design, with a ring connecting the four straight arms.

4. Emerging from the Lady's Well enclosure, turn left.

Escape Route: Head straight ahead to Holystone village.

5. Cross the stile you reach and carry straight on, along the side of the field. Continue through the next gateway, and two gap stiles in quick succession, until you arrive at a pair of metal gates. Descend the four steps.

You are following the waymarking to Wood Hall Farm.

☺ The hills in the distance are the Cheviots. They have a curiously rounded shape because they are made of solidified lava that poured from the

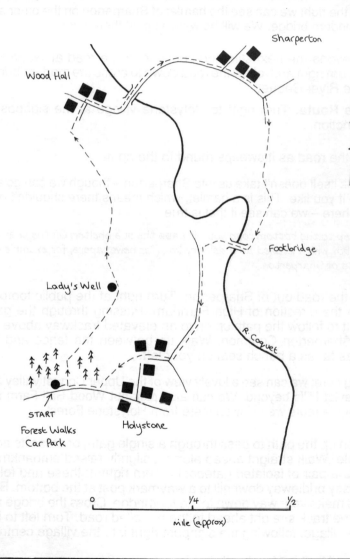

WALK 5;
HOLYSTONE

Sharperton

Wood Hall

N

Footbridge

Lady's Well

R. Coquet

↑↑↑↑↑↑
↑↑↑↑↑

START
Forest Walks
Car Park   Holystone

0   ¼   ½

mile (approx)

ancient Cheviot volcano. It has, of course, been extinct for millions of years.

6. Negotiate the next gap stile, and bear left to walk along the edge of the pasture.

☺ Over to the right we can see the hamlet of Sharperton on the other side of the modern bridge. We will be walking past there later.

7. Pass beyond the next stile and continue to the road at Wood Hall Farm. Turn right and follow the road down to cross the modern bridge over the River Coquet.

Escape Route: Turn right to Holystone village at the signposted road junction.

8. Follow the road as it sweeps round to the right.

☺ The walk itself doesn't take us into Sharperton – though we can go and explore if you like. This is a hamlet, which means there shouldn't be a church here – we can see if that is true.

If you keep to the bottom road you will pass the bus shelter. On the seat is a wooden box which is used as a delivery box (for newspapers, for example) for residents of Sharperton.

9. Follow the road out of Sharperton. Turn right at the public footpath sign, in the direction of High Farnham. Passing through the gate, bear left to follow the path up on to an elevated trackway above the damp Sharperton Common. Walk up between the fence and the trees, as far as a bench seat on your left.

☺ Pausing here, we can see a lovely view of the Upper Coquet valley and the Cheviot Hills beyond. We can also pick out Wood Hall Farm and some of the route we followed there from Holystone Forest.

10. Carry on up the path to pass through a single gate, or cross its adjacent stile. Walk straight ahead along a slightly raised embankment towards a pair of isolated gateposts. Turn right at these and follow the grassy bridleway downhill to a waymark post at the bottom. Bear left and make your way down to the footbridge. Cross the bridge and follow the track straight ahead to the metalled road. Turn left to Holystone village, following the signpost right into the village centre.

Q: The speed limit is 15mph – is that for everyone?

A: No – just for military vehicles through the village.

11. In the village centre, avoid the temptation to turn left. Instead, press straight on down the lane that leads to the back of the row of cottages. Then go straight through the gate in front of you, between the hen houses, and make your way to, and then over, the stile. Walk obliquely left to cross a further stile, and then turn right up the metalled lane to the Holystone Forest Walks car park.

The Cheviots

Other Places of Interest in the Area

Harbottle

A couple of miles further up Coquetdale, towards Alwinton, is the small linear village of Harbottle where there is a ruined castle. There is also a tea-shop (Coquet Crafts) with a garden.

Rothbury

The market town of Rothbury is the commercial centre of Upper Coquetdale. There is a variety of shops and of refreshment opportunities in its cafés, pubs and hotels. The famous Cragside estate is nearby. Laid out by the inventor and industrialist Lord Armstrong in the 19th century, Cragside's grounds are famous for the early summer rhododendrons. The house itself was the first in the world to be lit by electricity, powered by water using a system Armstrong designed himself. The National Trust, its current owners, have restored the estate. Telephone (01669) 620333 for details of opening hours.

Alwinton

For information about Alwinton, the last village in England, see the next walk.

6. ALWINTON

Nestled in the Cheviot Hills of northern Northumberland, Alwinton is a small rural settlement at the end of the minor road which wends along upper Coquetdale from the market town of Rothbury. Beyond Alwinton there are no more villages, though the ancient road of Clennell Street – followed by the early part of this walk – leads on into the hills, where there are abandoned settlements from the past.

Alwinton, then, is on something of a frontier – the edge of the wilderness. However, in some respects, the rounded hills of the Cheviots present a gentle aspect of the wild. Their gentle curves result from ancient lava flows emanating from the long extinct Cheviot volcano and give a very characteristic look to the area.

Starting Point:	Alwinton, National Park car park (Grid ref. NT 919063)
Distance:	5 miles
Terrain:	Mostly on unsurfaced paths. There is an initial climb up Clennell Street's rather rocky trackway, but thereafter no steep rises.
Map:	OS Pathfinder 499 Harbottle or Outdoor Leisure map 16, The Cheviot Hills
Public Toilets:	Alwinton, car park
Refreshments:	Alwinton, Rose and Thistle Inn
Pushchairs:	Apart from the lanes immediately around Alwinton village, this is not a route for pushchairs.

☞ You should pass most of these. See how many you can spot:

☐ a wooden footbridge

☐ a silo

☐ a Northumberland National Park curlew symbol

☐ a drystone wall

☐ a gully cut by a stream

☐ a round hill

☐ a sheep with brown wool

☐ a black-faced sheep with blue marking

☐ a line of telegraph poles

☐ a motorcyclist

Near Alwinton

1. Start from the car park and walk back down the lane to the T-junction in the village centre.

☺ The pub in Alwinton is called the Rose and Thistle. Alwinton is the last village in England. Over the hills is Scotland. So, since the rose is the flower of England and the thistle of Scotland, the pub has quite an appropriate name.

2. Turn left and then almost immediately follow the direction indicated by the public footpath sign to Clennell Street.

☺ Clennell Street is not a street like a town street. It is a rough track along the line of an ancient routeway. Roads left behind by the Romans are often called street – Dere Street, for example, is followed through Corbridge by the modern A68.

3. Cross the small wooden footbridge over Hosedon Burn and turn left, following the public bridleway towards Clennell Street and the Border Bridge.

Q: Look at this sign. How far away is Scotland?

A: 8 miles

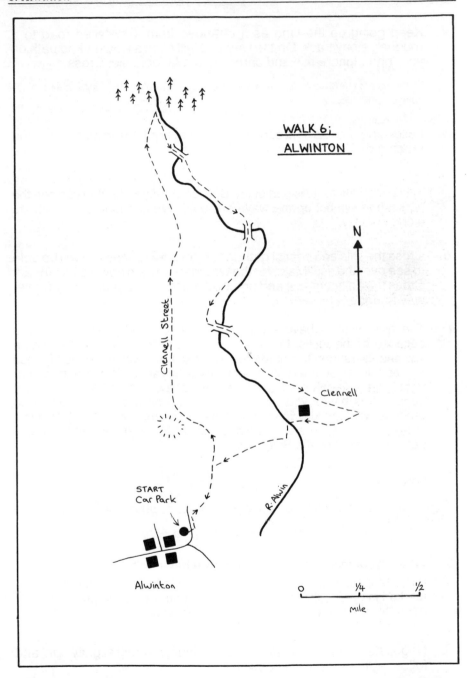

WALK 6;
ALWINTON

N

Clennell Street

Clennell

R. Alwin

START
Car Park

Alwinton

0   ¼   ½

mile

4. Keep going up the lane as it changes from a metalled road to a rougher, stony track. On the way you will pass a waymarked path on your right. Ignore this and carry on to a ladder stile. Cross.

To the left is the hill on which an ancient castle was built. You may decide to venture up and explore this site. The route carries straight on.

5. Follow the path as it sweeps round to the right. Keep going until you reach a divide in the way where there is a waymark post. Bear right towards a stile adjacent to a single hurdle gate.

☺ This part of the route is part of the Border County Ride. You can see the horseshoe symbol on the waymark post. We can look out for others along our way.

6. Cross the stile and bear slightly left. After a few paces you will be able to see over the rise. Make for the waymarked gate now visible ahead. Cross the adjacent stile and proceed along the evident grassy bridleway ahead.

☺ The hills of the Cheviots are unusually rounded in shape. This is because of the rocks. Millions of years ago the Cheviot itself was a volcano. Lava from this hardened to make rock, which produced these curved hilltops as it was weathered over the ages. The stream on our right is very steeply cut into its narrow valley. If you look on the outer banks of its bends you can see where it has undercut its banks to produce what are known as river cliffs. In the middle of the stream is a small island, called an eyot, which is made of stones and pebbles deposited there by the River Alwin.

7. Keep going.

☺ Look out on the left for a ruined, round, stone sheep pen.

This is marked on the OS Pathfinder map (Grid ref. 922081).

Q: What colour marking do the sheep here have? Why?
A: Blue. To distinguish them from sheep owned by other farmers, marked in other colours. Because the sheep are free to graze the open fell, they may otherwise become mixed up.

8. Negotiate the gate you reach and continue, bearing slightly right and following the grassy way downhill.

☺ The trees ahead are part of a plantation. That means that people have deliberately planted them. You can tell this because of the straightness of the edge of the plantation and of the rows of trees themselves.

9. So, you come down to a gate. Turn hard right on to the lane and walk away from the forest. Carry on until you cross a bridge over the Alwin.

Q: What is unusual about this bridge?

A: There are no sides. The bridge is not used very often, and mostly by people who know their way so sides are not really needed to stop traffic falling off.

10. Keep walking along the gravel track, across two more footbridges, as far as the farm buildings of Clennell, where the track divides. Bear left of a corner in the drystone wall and walk towards the single stone cottage to pass through the adjacent pair of metal gates. Walk straight ahead, parallel to the line of trees on your left, until the path bends left and passes through a gateway into open country.

☺ This caravan site is at Clennell. Remember the track we began on was called Clennell Street. We will need to almost double back on ourselves, and walk through the caravan site. It is a public right of way though, so that means we are allowed to do that.

11. Continue on for a few metres, until you can turn right without wetting your feet, and then walk back towards the drystone wall, making for a single wooden gate set in the wall, a little to the left. Pass through the gate and walk straight ahead through the caravan site, bearing left of Clennell Hall to a junction on the driveway. Turn right – signposted 'Reception' – and walk on as far as a tall hedge of conifers. Turn left in front of these trees and pass through the old iron gate ahead.

☺ We will need to cross this cattle grid. It is there to stop freely grazing animals from wandering Into the grounds of the hall.

12. Bear left across the cattle grid and then right to a footbridge. Cross.

Q: How far is it back to Alwinton now?

A: ¾ mile (waymark sign).

13. Having crossed the footbridge, turn left and walk to the top of the rise before following the waymarking right to a stile. Cross the stile and walk straight on across the pasture to negotiate the stile at the other end. Turn left down Clennell Street and retrace your early steps back to Alwinton.

Other Places of Interest in the Area

Harbottle and Rothbury

For information about these local places of interest, see the end of the previous walk.

Holystone

Full details are supplied in walk number 5.

7. HOLY ISLAND

Holy Island is so-called because of its Benedictine monastery – now in ruins. It is the largest of the Farne Islands off the Northumberland coast – its alternative name is Lindisfarne. The island is connected to the mainland by a causeway which is only open when the tide is quite low. You will need to check the tide times in advance of setting out – remember to also check for your return. Tourist Information Centres such as the one at Seahouses can help (tel. 01665 720885).

The Museum of Island Life is open between Easter and October; it recreates the way of life of a fishing family living and working from 18th-century Hillcroft Cottage. For details, telephone its sister facility – the Seahouses Marine Life and Fishing Centre on 01665 721257 or 720712.

The walk is a circular one around about half of the island, taking in the main sights of the priory ruins, the harbour and the castle along the way.

Starting Point: Car park, Holy Island village (Grid ref. NU 127422)

Distance: 3½ miles

Terrain: Varies, but mostly on unsurfaced paths. The climb up from the ruins is quite steep.

Map: OS Pathfinder 452, Beal/Holy Island

Public Toilets: Holy Island village

Refreshments: Holy Island village

Pushchairs: Though the lanes around the village are suitable, the full circular route is not.

☞ You should pass most of these. See how many you can spot:

☐ a bottle of Lindisfarne Mead

☐ a church with a spire

☐ a dyke

☐ a lobster pot

☐ a castle

☐ a lime kiln

☐ a pond

☐ sand dunes

☐ a ruined monastery

1. Start from the car park in Holy Island village. Turn right out of the exit and walk down to the T-junction. Turn left and walk straight on to the church grounds.

You may want to take this chance to visit the priory remains.

☺ There was first a monastery here in the 7th century. Monks who came from another island – Iona, which is off the west coast of Scotland – founded it. However, this first monastery was made of wood, and the stone ruins we can see date from about 950 years ago.

2. From the ruins, head back to the church. Turn left, and follow the path to a single gate. Pass through it and turn left to walk along the track. At the end, head up the path to your left.

☺ This ridge of rock is a dyke. It sticks up because it is made of resistant rock, which solidified from molten material underground millions of years ago.

3. Where there is a lower section to the ridge, bear left and then walk to your right along the gravel path.

☺ The harbour here is used by boats catching crab and lobster. Perhaps we could try some crab sandwiches in the village when we have finished the walk.

4. At the junction of tracks, turn right.

☺ We can now see the castle ahead of us. It was built in the 16th century – so it isn't really very old for Northumberland! By that time the monastery was closed and the island had become more important for the defence of the mainland – or rather to stop any potential invaders from using it as a base.

4. Pass through a kissing gate and bear left to walk around the bottom of the castle mount. Keep following the path as it swings leftward. Pass through another kissing gate and walk on to a junction of tracks.

Escape Route: Turn left along the lane to return to Holy Island village.

5. Carry straight on.

☺ The lake on our left is called the Lough. It is freshwater, not salty like the sea.

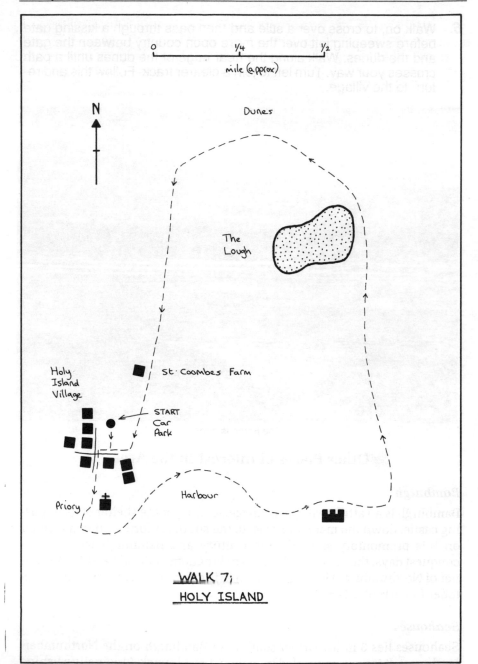

WALK 7;
HOLY ISLAND

6. Walk on, to cross over a stile and then pass through a kissing gate before sweeping left over the more open country between the gate and the dunes. Walk along the near edge of the dunes until a path crosses your way. Turn left to join a clearer track. Follow this and return to the village.

The Farne Islands

Other Places of Interest in the Area

Bamburgh

Bamburgh is an attractive, green village nestling in the shelter of its imposing castle, down the mainland coast to the south,. A fortification has stood on this promontory since the 6th century and Bamburgh was, in pre-conquest days, the capital of the ancient kingdom of Bernicia – the forerunner of Northumbria. The castle is open to the public daily from April to October (tel. 01668 214515).

Seahouses

Seahouses lies 3 miles further south than Bamburgh on the Northumberland coast. It is well signposted from the A1 at Alnwick. Originally a fishing village, the settlement has developed a tourism-based economy over the last 25 years or so. Fishing itself is now much curtailed and the harbour not as busy as it was. Nevertheless, there are boats to be seen all year and the summer season brings a marked increase in activity.

The Farne Islands

These rocky islands, formed of resistant Whin Sill, lie just offshore. Inner Farne is clearly visible from the beach. A seabird sanctuary and grey seal breeding ground, the islands may be visited by boat from Seahouses harbour.

8. BAMBURGH

Bamburgh is a green village on the north Northumberland coast, nestling in the shade of its imposing castle. A fortification has stood on this prominent site since the 6th century. In those days, Bamburgh was the capital of the ancient kingdom of Bernicia, and later the site of the coronations of the kings of Northumbria. The present castle dates from Norman times, although it was substantially remodelled in the 19th century. It is open to the public and includes the Armstrong industrial heritage museum. Telephone (01668) 2142515. In the village itself there is also the Grace Darling Museum — dedicated to the heroine who saved sailors from the wreck of the Forfarshire off the Farne Islands in 1838. There is, however, no telephone.

Starting Point:	Bamburgh car park (Grid ref. NU 184349)
Distance:	5 miles
Terrain:	Beach on the way out, field paths and lanes on the return leg.
Map:	OS Pathfinder 465 Belford, Seahouses and Farne Islands
Public Toilets:	Bamburgh
Refreshments:	Bamburgh
Pushchairs:	The lanes around the village are suitable, but not the route itself.

☞ You should pass most of these. See how many you can spot:

☐ spiky marram grass

☐ shells

☐ seaweed

☐ a horse-rider

☐ a lifebelt

☐ a kite or a sandcastle

☐ a lighthouse

☐ seagulls

☐ a grass tennis court

☐ black and brown cattle

1. Start by walking out of the front of the car park and turning left towards the village.

To visit the village, simply turn left at the corner.

2. To follow this route, turn right at the corner of the road, on to the path which skirts the cricket field. Make for the base of the castle rock and follow the sandy path onto the beach. Turn right and keep walking.

☺ Look out for these places on our beach walk: Bamburgh Castle, the folded rock layers (called strata) of Greenhill rocks and the stone beach-side cottages at Monks House.

As you walk down the beach you will, at low tide, have a wide expanse at your disposal. At times of higher water, you may be more confined, possibly to the edge of the dunes themselves. In either event, you should enjoy a fine view of the Farne Islands which, although they may not look it, are some 1½ miles offshore. In the other direction, at least from the top of the dunes themselves, you can see as far as the Cheviots on a clear day.

☺ The island we can see is one of the Farnes. These islands are a bird sanctuary now but in the past were used by hermits, including St Cuthbert.

There are boat trips to and around the Farnes from Seahouses harbour, which you will reach later on the walk. The dunes you pass on your right as you approach Seahouses are St Aidan's Dunes.

3. Passing St Aidan's Dunes, you will come to the end of the beach walk. At the end, ascend a flight of steps up on to the links.

To extend the walk further by visiting Seahouses, turn left and walk along the top of the sea banks. See Walk 2 for further information.

Fun in the surf!

4. Turn right alongside the road and walk past the end of the houses. Beyond the first road junction, walk straight ahead on the landward side of the dunes. At the second, turn left and walk up the lane.

☺ The walled grounds here are those of Shoreston Hall.

5. Beyond the hall, turn right down a minor lane to pass South and North Cottages. Walk straight ahead until, having rounded a left-hand corner, you pass a ruin of on your left.

☺ This ruin is of Saddleshall.

6. Beyond Saddleshall, round two successive right-angled, right-hand corners to approach Fowberry. At the junction of lanes, turn right. Pass through the metal farm gate you reach and walk on to the next. Beyond it, walk along with the hedge on your left and turn right at the corner. Walk along the track, downwards, to another gate. Pass through and make your way up, along the path, to a wall ahead and a little over to your right. Follow the line of this wall to a track, which takes you beyond the end of a lane on your right.

☺ This is the lane leading to Greenhill Farm.

7. Keep on this track, over field boundaries on the way, until you approach the stone-built house of Red Barns. Walk along the front of the house and through the waymarked gate at the end. Continue the few metres to the intersection of tracks and then turn left to walk up to a stile on your right. Cross and walk up to, and along the front of, the cottages. Beyond the cottages, proceed to the top of the mound in the pasture ahead. Follow the path diagonally down to cross the stile to the roadside. Turn left to walk alongside the road to return to Bamburgh car park.

Other Places of Interest in the Area

Seahouses lies about 3 miles south of Bamburgh, still on the Northumberland coast. Originally a fishing village, the settlement has developed a tourism-based economy over the last 25 years or so. Fishing itself is now much curtailed and the harbour not as busy as it was. Nevertheless, there are boats to be seen all year and the summer season brings a marked increase in activity.

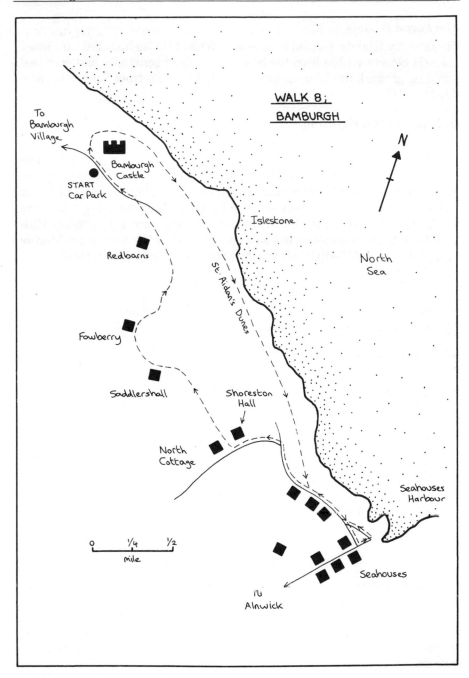

WALK 8;
BAMBURGH

N

To
Bamburgh
Village

Bamburgh
Castle

START
Car Park

Islestone

North
Sea

Redbarns

St. Aidan's Dunes

Fowberry

Saddlershall

Shoreston
Hall

North
Cottage

Seahouses
Harbour

0   ¼   ½
mile

To
Alnwick

Seahouses

The Farne Islands

These rocky islands, formed of resistant Whin Sill, lie just offshore. Inner Farne is clearly visible from the beach. A seabird sanctuary and grey seal breeding ground, the islands may be visited by boat from Seahouses harbour.

Holy Island (Lindisfarne)

Further to the north is the island of Lindisfarne, its castle and ruined 7th-century monastery. Connected to the mainland by causeway, it is accessible only at low tide and you will need to check the times before setting out. Tourist Information Centres such as the one at Seahouses can help. The Museum of Island Life is open between Easter and October; it recreates the way of life of a fishing family living and working from 18th-century Hillcroft Cottage. The museum is a sister enterprise of the Seahouses Marine Life Museum, and further information may be obtained from there.

9. NORTH SHIELDS AND TYNEMOUTH

This walk begins by the River Tyne in North Shields and takes in the Fish Quay of that town as well as the village and seafront at Tynemouth, where there are golden sandy beaches. Culminating in the former fishing village of Cullercoats, the route is unusually not completely circular on foot in that much of the return involves a short ride on the Tyneside Metro supertram system.

Starting Point:	New Quay, North Shields (Grid ref. NZ 355678)
Distance:	4 miles
Terrain:	On surfaced paths for the most part, with a short grassy stretch by the Collingwood Monument and an optional beach section.
Map:	OS Pathfinder 549 Newcastle upon Tyne and 536 Whitley Bay
Public Toilets:	North Shields, Fish Quay and Tynemouth
Refreshments:	A variety of cafés, pubs and takeaways at the Fish Quay, in Tynemouth, and in Cullercoats.
Pushchairs:	This is possible, though it is a bit of a push up the bank by the Collingwood Monument and you may need to circumnavigate Tynemouth Station because of the steps up to the footbridge.

☞ You should pass most of these. See how many you can spot:

☐   a ferry

☐   a wooden dolly

☐   a fishing boat

☐   a comedian's statue

☐   an old fort

☐   an admiral's monument

☐   a ruined castle

☐   a Metro train

☐   a glass-roofed station

☐   an aquarium

1. Start in the cobbled square of the New Quay.

☺ From here we can look over the River Tyne. The town on the other side is South Shields and the ferry, which connects here and there, sails from the New Quay. Can you spot it?

2. Walk past the Porthole pub.

Formerly the Golden Fleece, the Porthole was once notorious for all manner of dockside goings-on, including shanghaiing of sailors. The actual porthole in the door was taken from the Ark Royal. The first of numerous potential refreshment stops along this walk, the Porthole offers bar meals and real ale.

3. Continue straight ahead along the flat road until you pass the Prince of Wales Tavern (old Wooden Dolly) on your right.

☺ On the wall is a painted wooden dolly. It is 8ft (about 2½ metres) high. Sailors used to cut a piece of wood from the doll before setting sail – to bring them good luck.

4. Keep walking to the Fish Quay itself.

☺ The Fish Quay is where the once much larger North Shields fishing fleet lands its catch. There are fish merchants all along here selling fish to customers and to shops all over the country.

5. Walk along the quay until you reach the covered section. Head to the left of this and look out for a stairway between the buildings on your left. Climb the stairs to the top and turn left along the river view walkway, towards the white tower of the disused High Light.

☺ The High Light and its twin on the quayside (the Low Light) used to be used to guide ships into the Tyne. Sea captains could line the lights up into a straight line – one behind the other and know they were steering a safe course into the river. There are some notoriously dangerous rocks (called the Black Middens) at the mouth of the Tyne. Sailors obviously wanted to steer clear of them.

6. Carry on past the High Light as far as Dockwray Square.

☺ In the middle of the square is a statue. It is of a comedian called Stan Laurel who was very famous in the early part of the 20th century as an actor in silent films. His partner was called Oliver Hardy, and their black and white Laurel and Hardy movies are still very funny. Stan Laurel was

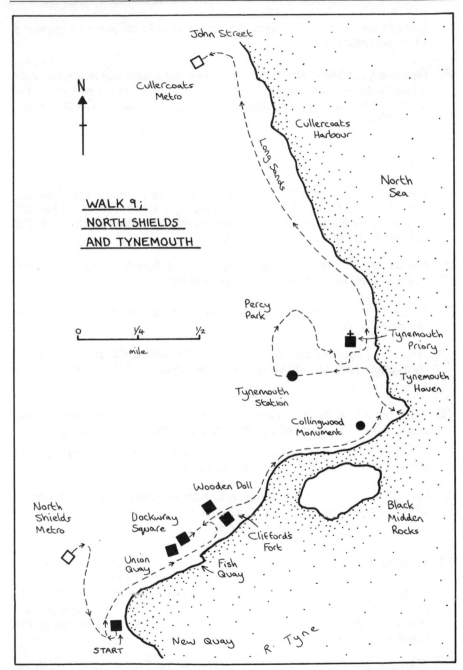

John Street

N

Cullercoats
Metro

Cullercoats
Harbour

North
Sea

Long Sands

WALK 9;
NORTH SHIELDS
AND TYNEMOUTH

Percy
Park

0   ¼   ½

mile

Tynemouth
Priory

Tynemouth
Station

Tynemouth
Haven

Collingwood
Monument

Wooden Doll

North
Shields
Metro

Dockwray
Square

Clifford's
Fort

Black
Midden
Rocks

Union
Quay

Fish
Quay

New Quay

R. Tyne

START

brought up here in Dockwray Square and only moved to Hollywood when he grew up.

7. Retrace your steps along the river view walkway, but this time walk on as far as the Wooden Doll pub. Turn right and walk down this stair-case to the quay. Turn left and then right, just in front of Dolphin Fish-eries. Walk on to Clifford's Fort.

☺ This fort is named after Lord Clifford. It was built over 300 years ago and used for cannon which guarded the entrance to the Tyne.

8. Pass Clifford's Fort and turn left into the next yard of the Fish Market. Pass through this and turn right, keeping the herring smokeries on your right all the time, until you reach the path which leads on to the actual mouth of the Tyne.

☺ Herring are fish which can be smoked over a slow-burning fire to make kippers. That is what these buildings are for.

9. Follow the waymarked path ahead in the direction of Tynemouth Pri-ory and Castle.

☺ The monument we can see is to Admiral Lord Collingwood. Born in Newcastle, Collingwood served with Nelson at the Battle of Trafalgar in 1805.

10. Walk on along the riverside promenade until you take one of the paths which slope up leftwards to the Collingwood Monument.

It doesn't matter which path you take – so long as it isn't the last one! You may let the children run on here, up to the monument.

Q: Run up to the monument. When was Admiral Collingwood born and where is he buried?

A: 1748 and St Paul's Cathedral, London.

11. Walk to the right of the monument and down the grassy slope be-yond. At the bottom, take the path to your right as far as the access road to Tynemouth Haven. Turn right up to the vantage point, which overlooks it, and then return to the bottom of the dip, where a path leads off right to the pier. Keep going straight ahead, up the hill, to the entrance to the priory and castle.

☺ The headland has a commanding view over the Tyne's mouth and there have been fortifications here for as long as any one knows. The Priory itself has been here well over a thousand years – though it was rebuilt in the stones we now see before becoming ruined after the monastery was dissolved about 450 years ago.

You may want to break off from your walk to visit this English Heritage site, or return by car after you have completed the route.

12. Turn left into Tynemouth village. Walk the length of Front Street, crossing the road at the end into Huntingdon Place and then bearing left to walk down to Tynemouth Station.

☺ Tynemouth Station is used by the Tyneside Metro now. Later we will be going for a ride on one of its supertram trains. However, the station itself is much older. It is Victorian, which means it is about 100 years old. The station has been recently restored. Look at the glass roof.

Escape Route: Take the Metro to North Shields and then follow the directions given at the end of this walk, back to the New Quay.

13. Walk into the station and cross the footbridge to walk out the other side. Turn right up the lane. At the end, cross the road, turning left then right, past the nursery garden and into Percy Park. Walk down Percy Park to the seafront.

☺ Many streets in Tynemouth are called Percy something or other. This one is Percy Park. Percy is the family name of the Dukes of Northumberland who own much of the land on which Tynemouth is built. The triangular field here is called Sea Field. In days gone by it used to be used to graze cattle.

Of marginal significance is the fact that this author used to live in Percy Park – at number 53!

At the end of the street you will need to decide whether to walk down to the beach (the Long Sands) or stay on the path at the top of the Sea Banks.

14. Turn left and walk to Cullercoats.

☺ The village of Cullercoats was originally much smaller and a fishing village. In Cullercoats we can catch the train from the Metro station, back to North Shields. The old lifeboat station there is still recognisable. Keep a look-out for it.

The old lifeboat station is named and is at the corner of John Street.

15. From the harbour in Cullercoats, walk inland along John Street and then turn left down Station Road to the Metro. Catch the tram (one every 10 minutes) to North Shields – two stops. Alight at North Shields and walk up to the station exit. Turn hard right to walk along the side of the station building until you reach Borough Road, third on the left. Walk down Borough Road to return to the New Quay.

Other Places of Interest in the Area

Sea Life Centre, Tynemouth

The only real wet-weather attraction in Tynemouth. Sited on the seafront between Tynemouth village and Cullercoats, the Sea Life Centre is an aquarium featuring a walk-through tunnel surrounded by milling fish. There is a café and children's soft play. The Sea Life Centre (tel. 0191 257 6100) is open daily from 10am.

Whitley Bay

The next settlement north of Cullercoats is the seaside town of Whitley Bay, which is a little larger than Tynemouth and includes the Spanish City fairground. There is a good range of shops in the town and at the northern end is St Mary's Island with its landmark lighthouse – accessible on foot at low tide. This is open to the public, and there is also a visitor centre.

Wet'n'Wild

This indoor water theme attraction may be a good reward for active children for completing the walk. It is outside North Shields in the redeveloped Royal Quays area and is well signposted – from the A1058 Coast Road, for instance.

10. THE ROMAN WALL

Hadrian's Wall dates from the 2nd century AD, and marked the northern frontier of the Roman Empire in Britain. This walk takes you right alongside the stones, passing a ruined milecastle en route, and turning within striking distance of Housesteads Roman Fort to return to Steel Rigg along the Roman Military Way.

To reach Steel Rig by car, turn north from the B6318, opposite the Once Brewed National Park Centre, and drive three-quarters of a mile uphill.

Starting Point: Steel Rigg National Park car park (Grid ref. NY 751677)

Distance: 3½ or 6½ miles

Terrain: Sections of the outward route are steep and slippery in wet weather, though the return is easy going along an often grassy track.

Map: OS Pathfinder 546 Haltwhistle and Gilsland

Public Toilets: National Park Centre, Once Brewed – opposite the beginning of the lane which leads up to Steel Rigg.

Refreshments: Once Brewed Visitor Centre, Twice Brewed Inn

Pushchairs: The outward route in particular is certainly not suitable.

☞ You should pass most of these. See how many you can spot:

☐   a milecastle

☐   an old well

☐   tree roots crossing your path

☐   a lake

☐   a sycamore tree

☐   a National Trust emblem

☐   an acorn waymarker

☐   a boulder field

☐   sheep with blue markings

☐   black cattle

The Roman Wall

🙂 Go and look at the noticeboard about Hadrian's Wall.

Q: How high was the wall originally, and what date does the picture show?
A: 4½ metres and AD250.

1. Start by walking out of the car park at the opposite end to the car entrance. Follow the path to the remains and turn left to walk along with the stones on your right.

Q: How many courses (rows) high is the wall here?
A: 5

🙂 The stones have been laid without mortar because they are so regularly cut. It is over 1700 years since the original wall was built and many stones have been taken away over the centuries — to be used in local buildings.

2. Keep walking beside the wall. Go down the dip and climb the steep steps on the other side.

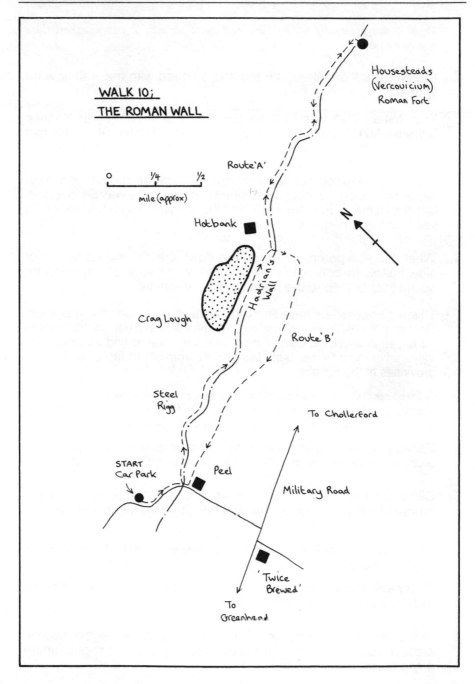

WALK 10;
THE ROMAN WALL

0   ¼   ½
mile (approx)

Housesteads
(Vercovicium)
Roman Fort

Route 'A'

Hotbank

Hadrian's Wall

Crag Lough

Route 'B'

Steel
Rigg

START
Car Park

Peel

To Chollerford

Military Road

'Twice
Brewed'

To
Greenhead

N

These steps are rocky, steep, long and quite slippery in wet weather. Care should be taken.

3. Cross the ladder stile at the top and proceed with the wall now on your left.

☺ The Roman Wall was built on the orders of the Emperor Hadrian between AD120 and 130. It was the northern frontier of the Roman Empire in Britain. We have now crossed to the Roman side of the wall. When we started we were on the Picts' side.

If you look ahead you can see how the wall was built along the top of a series of cliffs facing the Picts. This meant that it would be very difficult to attack the Romans from the north, and that the soldiers on the wall could see a long way north.

4. When the wall peters out, continue down the dip and up the other side. Follow the course of the wall now — still on your left, until you descend the next dip to the remains of a milecastle.

☺ This is a milecastle. These little forts were spaced along the wall every Roman mile (1620 metres) and a contingent of 32 Roman soldiers would be based in each. Actually, it would be very rare to find soldiers from Italy, never mind Rome itself. Most came from other, far away, frontier provinces of the Empire.

Children are likely to want to explore the ruins. A stile affords access. Indicate the gateway through the wall. This would be a point where trade could pass across the frontier under the scrutiny of the milecastle guards.

Escape Route 1: Turn right at the milecastle and then right again along the return route to Steel Rigg, via the cottage at Peel.

5. Climb the rise beyond the milecastle and continue to follow the course of the wall, keeping it to your left. The next steep, stepped descent brings you down to a well.

Appropriate care needs to be taken on the descent to the well. If children are running ahead, it would be a god idea to tell them to wait at the top.

Escape Route 2: Turn right at the well and then right again along the track to Peel Cottage, and thence to Steel Rigg.

6. At the well, cross the line of the wall and ascend the flagged path to cross a ladder stile. There is a second such stile to your right. Ignore it and press straight ahead.

☺ The cliffs here are very high so keep well away from the edge. The lake at the bottom is called Crag Lough.

7. The path will take you through a stretch of woodland to a ladder stile. Cross and walk on as far as the farm track. To the right is an acorn-marked ladder stile. Cross it, if the gate is closed.

8. Route A: Walk a few metres along the track and turn right at the way-mark sign, in the direction of Steel Rigg. Go up the rise until you can see the green Military Way straight ahead.

9. Route B: Cross the stile to the left of the farm track and follow the waymarked path to Housesteads Roman Fort. After your visit, re-trace your steps to this point.

The round trip would add 3 miles to your walk. This may be ambitious with children and so you may prefer to complete Route A and then visit Housesteads by car afterwards.

The following information for children applies to Route A.

☺ The path to Steel Rigg is along the Roman Military Way. The Roman frontier was more than just the wall. It was a military zone. The wall, which is on our right, was one edge. To our left was a large ditch called the Vallum, and between the two a corridor along which the soldiers could operate, completely separated from the local civilians of the time. The Military Way we are walking along would have been the Romans' supply route, parallel to the wall itself. You can tell they designed it – it's so straight!

10. Follow the Military Way straight ahead. Cross a stile next to a gate and continue to negotiate a second. The track begins to drop down into a gully and you will recognise the well you passed earlier – on your right.

This is where Escape Route 2 brings you on the return route.

11. Carry on along the path straight ahead, resisting any temptation to bear left. Cross a ladder stile and carry on until you round a cliff on your right to begin to walk up to a cottage.

This is Peel.

12. Cross the stile to the right of the cottage. Walk straight ahead to the next stile and cross it, too. Turn right up the metalled lane, rounding the bend to return to the car park at Steel Rigg.

Other Places of Interest in the Area

Housesteads Roman Fort

Known to the Romans themselves as Vercovicium, Housesteads is the most completely preserved Roman fort in Britain and lies 3 miles east of Once Brewed, along the B6318. It is open daily (tel. 01434 344363).

Vindolanda

Vindolanda was an earlier fort built on the Stanegate – the frontier before Hadrian's Wall was built. The museum at Vindolanda vividly recreates life on the Roman frontier and helps children's understanding of the remains. There is a reconstruction of a section of the Wall and a tower. Vindolanda (tel. 01434 344727) is open daily from March to October, and weekends in November and February.

Hexham

The market town of Hexham is the principal settlement on Tynedale. Saturday is a good day to visit for a bit of country town bustle. There is a small market and numerous shops, from chic little boutiques and delicatessens to Robbs department store. Midweek, the market is held on Tuesdays. The abbey dates from the 12th century and has an older, Saxon crypt.

11. ALLEN BANKS

The National Trust property of Allen Banks allows a children-friendly stroll through the woods beside the River Allen, including two swaying suspension bridges en-route. The walk takes you as far as the beauty spot of Plankey Mill and affords the opportunity of a visit to Briarwoods Nature Reserve.

Starting Point:	Allen Banks National Trust car park and picnic site (Grid ref. NY 797640)
Distance:	3¼ miles
Terrain:	Mostly unsurfaced woodland paths.
Map:	OS Pathfinder 546 Haltwhistle and Gilsland
Public Toilets:	Allen Banks car park and picnic site
Refreshments:	There is a picnic site, otherwise the nearest refreshments are in Bardon Mill village.
Pushchairs:	Only suitable as far as the first footbridge.

☞ You should pass most of these. See how many you can spot:

☐ a rhododendron bush
☐ logs
☐ leaves of oak and beech
☐ moss
☐ rapids
☐ a sandstone cliff
☐ a National Trust emblem
☐ a suspension bridge
☐ another suspension bridge
☐ molehills

1. Start from the National Trust car park and picnic site.

The car park is what was the kitchen garden of Ridley Hall. Glancing round at the sheltering walls, one can perhaps imagine how it would have been.

2. Leave the car park along the path past the information board at the opposite end from the car entrance. Follow the path to the first way-marker.

Q: We are following the brown route to Plankey Mill. Which way should
     we go?

A: Left.

3.   Bear left at the fork and stick to the riverside path all the way.

☺ The channel of the River Allen is boulder-strewn. The river only moves
   these boulders when it is in flood, after a storm or snowmelt.

4.   Coming to a suspended footbridge, continue straight ahead.

Escape Route: Cross the footbridge and turn left to follow the path
on the opposite bank back towards the car park.

5.   Climb the rather slithery slope to a crossing of paths. Bear left, along
     the main path closer to the river. Reaching a more open spot on the
     inside of a river bend, pause.

☺ On the inside of the bend we can see a shingle beach. This is material
   left behind by the river because its current is diverted towards the outer
   bank, where you can see how it has undercut the bank to form a small,
   steep river cliff.

6.   Follow the path round to the right. Keep going, following the brown
     arrows, until you enter the Northumberland Wildlife Trust's Briar-
     wood Banks Nature Reserve. Continue along the path until you
     reach a footbridge with white railings.

To the right of the footbridge is an information board about Briarwood Banks.
You might encourage the children to go and read it. In spring there are many
wild flowers to be found, and you may care to take a detour around the marked
route.

☺ Briarwood is one of England's ancient woodlands which have remained
   unfelled by people since trees returned following the end of the last Ice
   Age. The wood includes ash, wych elm, sessile oak and birch, as well as
   old yew trees and hazel. There are some pictures on the board to help us
   identify them — perhaps we can try to do that.

7.   Cross the white bridge. Take the stepped path straight up and
     ahead, bearing right where it divides. From the top of the rise, take
     the steps down to cross the suspension bridge to Plankey Mill.

This bridge does tend to sway as you cross. Smaller children may need some re-

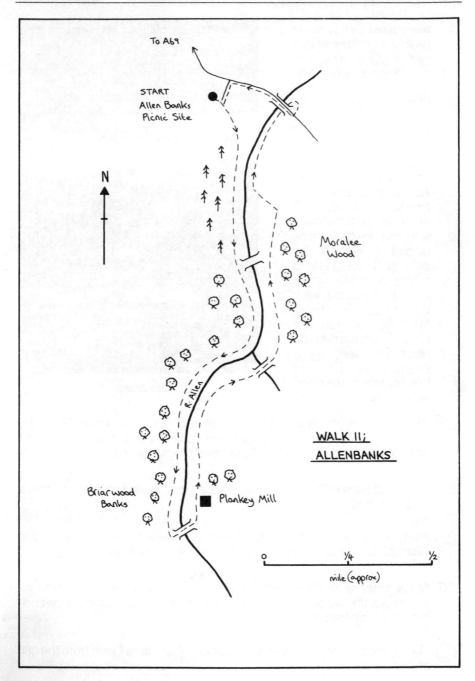

To A69

START
Allen Banks
Picnic Site

N

Moralee
Wood

R. Allen

WALK II;
ALLENBANKS

Briarwood
Banks

Plankey Mill

0   ¼   ½

mile (approx)

assurance. The opposite bank is a popular beauty spot where a picnic stop may be made by the river.

8. Having crossed the bridge, walk straight ahead to the metal gate. Pass through, and follow the lane up and round to the left. As the lane begins to sweep right, leave it and turn left to follow a waymarked track downhill. Cross the stile and continue to cross a ladder stile over a drystone wall. Continue, following the fence on your left until a waymarker directs you left, via a couple of hairpin bends, to a more riverside route.

Allen Banks

☺ It looks as though the path has been altered here. There is a sign on the fenced-off section about a dangerous edge. The river has undercut the original path and made it too dangerous to walk along.

9. Cross the next stile and walk along the path, between the river and a drystone wall.

☺ Along here are some of the trees mentioned on the Briarwood information board. Keep an eye out for yew and hazel, as well as gorse.

10. At the outer bank of the next bend, which you will recognise from earlier, cross the wooden footbridge and walk left and upwards, wending your way between large boulders.

☺ These boulders have very straight edges. They have fallen from the cliff on our right.

11. Keep going until the path divides by a stone seat. Follow the brown waymarking, straight ahead.

Along this section you may notice a purple-arrowed route up some steps to the right. This is a possible detour to the tarn in Moralee Wood, which rejoins the walk later.

12. Where the brown waymarking points downhill, ignore it. Walk straight ahead, keeping to the higher path.

At the next fork the way from the tarn in Moralee Wood rejoins the route.

13. Take the left fork here. Begin to dip down and continue along as the path widens to a green track. Follow it round as it bends left and cross the stile to walk along the edge of the field, passing a recessed gate on your right, until you join a larger track. Turn right and follow the track all the way to, and under, the road bridge. Turn right and walk away from the riverbank to a single wooden gate. Go through, and turn right to cross the bridge to return to the car park.

Other Places of Interest in the Area

Housesteads Roman Fort

Known to the Romans as Vercovicium, Housesteads is the most completely preserved Roman fort in Britain and lies 3 miles east of Once Brewed, along the B6318. From Allen Banks, turn briefly west along the A69 and then follow the Vindolanda signs. It is open daily (tel. 01434 344363).

Vindolanda

Vindolanda is between Allen Banks and Housesteads. It was an earlier fort built on the Stanegate – the frontier before Hadrian's Wall was built. The museum at Vindolanda vividly recreates life on the Roman frontier and helps children's understanding of the remains. There is a reconstruction of a section of the wall and a tower. Vindolanda (tel. 01434 344727) is open daily from March to October, and weekends in November and February.

Hexham

The market town of Hexham is the principal settlement in Tynedale. Saturday is a good day to visit for a bit of country town bustle. There is a small market and numerous shops, from chic little boutiques and delicatessens to Robbs department store. Midweek, the market is held on Tuesdays. The abbey dates from the 12th century, but has an older, Saxon crypt.

12. DIPTON MILL

Dipton Mill is the tiniest of hamlets. To all intents and purposes there is only the pretty country pub next to the bridge. It is located just 2 miles to the south of the market town of Hexham, but there is a real away from it all feel to the place.

To take full advantage of your day you will probably want to avail yourself of the pub's hospitality. In summer the beer garden to the rear will be your best bet with children. Out of season, or in wet weather, you may initially be anxious about the 'No children in the bar' sign by the front door. There is a back sitting room with a real fire and bar billiard table where we actually felt more relaxed as a family and better able to enjoy the good food and real ale which draw people from miles around to the Dipton Mill.

The walk itself is largely through woods, with a return along a quiet, metalled lane.

Starting Point: The Dipton Mill pub (Grid ref. NY 929609)
Distance: 2½ miles
Terrain: Mostly on woodland paths, which can be muddy, and occasionally narrow and slippery. The walk returns to Dipton Mill along a metalled lane.
Map: OS Pathfinder 547 Hexham and Haydon Bridge
Toilets: The Dipton Mill pub (for customers)
Refreshments: The Dipton Mill
Pushchairs: The metalled lane between the pub and Windy Hill forms the return leg of the route and the only section suitable for pushchairs.

☞ You should pass most of these. See how many you can spot:
☐ a stone bridge
☐ an old lamp
☐ a sycamore tree
☐ ferns
☐ a waterfall
☐ wild honeysuckle
☐ a drystone wall
☐ toadstools
☐ a blackberry bush
☐ a silver birch tree

Dipton Mill

1. Start as though emerging from the front door of the pub. Turn left and walk over the bridge to turn left again over the waymarked stile and into the woods. Walk on along the woodland path until you cross a stile. Look out for a fork in the paths and take the right-hand uphill route, bearing left after a little – keeping to the main path.

☺ The stream we are walking alongside is called West Dipton Burn. As we go through the wood, look at the bends, or meanders, in the stream's course.

Q: What difference can you see between the banks on the outer and inner parts of the bends?

A: The outer banks are steeper than the inner ones.

☺ The outer banks are called river cliffs and the inner bends have slip-off slopes. The outer ones are steep because they take the full force of the stream as it rounds the bend and this wears them away. On the inner bank, however, the stream flows only slowly and the slope is very gentle.

Along this stretch of the walk paths are not signed. Sticking to the main path, not venturing down to the water's edge, not straying out of sight of it, should be your rule of thumb. The children may well enjoy the exploring aspect of this!

2. Emerging beside a field, keep to the path just left of the fence and right of the trees. Cross a low hurdle stile on your way to the far end of the field. At the divide of the ways there, follow the woodland path, West Dipton Burn always on your left, until you reach a footbridge with white railings. Cross it.

Shortly before reaching the footbridge, the path briefly becomes narrow and rocky. Small children may well need some support for this short stretch.

3. Walk up the path on the opposite side. At the top, follow the grassy, near-tunnel of the green lane to the road junction. Turn left and walk along the lane.

☺ Look out for some nurseries on the right along here.

Q: What are they called?

A: Shield Green nurseries.

4. Follow the lane back to Dipton Mill.

☺ There is a funny sign above the pub doorway.

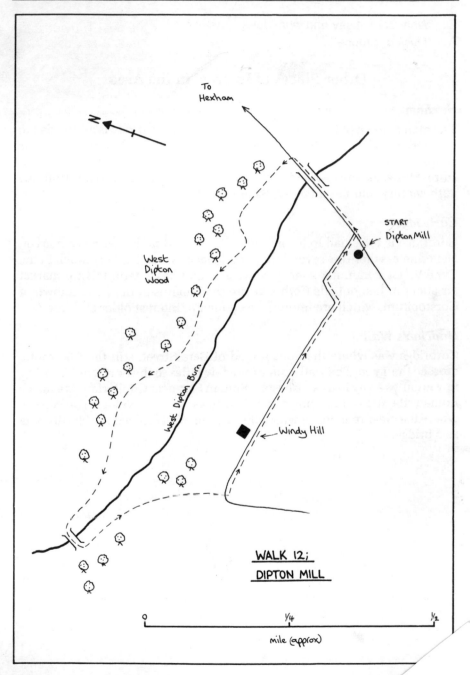

To Hexham

N

West Dipton Wood

West Dipton Burn

START Dipton Mill

Windy Hill

WALK 12;
DIPTON MILL

0   ¼   ½
mile (approx)

Q: What does it say and what does it mean?
A: 'Duck or grouse'!

Other Places of Interest in the Area

Hexham

The market town of Hexham is just 2 miles away. Saturday is a good day to
visit for a bit of country town bustle. There is a small market and numerous
shops, from chic little boutiques and delicatessens to Robbs department
store. Midweek, the market is held on Tuesdays. The abbey dates from the
12th century, but has an older, Saxon crypt.

Corbridge

Corbridge is too small to be properly a town, and no longer has a market.
Nevertheless there are several shops and places to eat. It is very much in the
Tyne Valley commuter zone of Newcastle and has a definitely up-market
air about it. Just outside Corbridge are the remains of the Roman town of
Corstopitum, which are impressive enough to interest older children.

Hadrian's Wall

Corbridge was where the Roman road of Dere Street, still the A68 route,
crossed the Tyne. The wall itself runs a few miles to the north, but is only a
few minutes away in a car. Chesters Roman Fort near Chollerford is a major
Roman site, with a museum to visit as well as ruins to explore. You can see
where the clear remains of where the Roman Wall crossed the North Tyne
as a bridge.

13. CAUSEY ARCH

Causey Arch is the world's oldest surviving railway bridge – built in 1725 to carry waggons of coal on wooden rails from nearby Tanfield Colliery to the Tyne to be loaded onto colliers and shipped to London (coals from Newcastle). The waggons ran down to the Tyne by gravity and were hauled back up by horses.

Causey Arch is well signposted. It stands close to the A6076 Stanley to Sunniside road. There is a picnic area, and the bridge itself spans a magnificent, wooded gorge, through which snake numerous pathways. This walk allows you to view and cross the bridge, explore the gorge and some of the surrounding countryside, and see the steam Tanfield Railway, which has a station at Causey Arch.

Starting Point:	Causey Arch picnic area (Grid ref. NZ 206562)
Distance:	2$\frac{1}{4}$ or 3$\frac{1}{4}$ miles
Terrain:	The short route is entirely on prepared pathways so the going is fairly easy. However, the paths are not metalled and can still be muddy following damp weather. The extension section is across fields for much of the way.
Map:	OS Pathfinder 561 Consett and 562 Chester-le-Street and Washington.
Public Toilets:	Causey Arch picnic area
Refreshments:	Causey Arch Inn or at Andrew's House Station on the Tanfield Railway.
Pushchairs:	The shorter route is suitable, though the stretch from the Arch to the top of the gorge is a little challenging at times.

☞ You should pass most of these. See how many you can spot:

- ☐ a goose
- ☐ an oak tree
- ☐ a steam engine
- ☐ a stone arch
- ☐ a railway signal
- ☐ an old truck
- ☐ a hay bale
- ☐ a hedge of holly
- ☐ a level-crossing

1. Start from the picnic area car park. From the toilet block, follow the waymarked pathway towards Causey Arch, without passing underneath the railway line. Continue into the woods.

Along the way are a number of information boards about the history of this heritage site. Look out for the first on your right.

Q: What is unusual about this hillside?
A: It is man-made.

☺ The embankment is over 100ft high, and was built to carry wooden coal waggons on their way from Causey Arch to the Tyne.

2. Walk on to a fork. Head left up the steps.

☺ The railway at the top of these steps is the Tanfield Railway. This is a restored steam railway. There is a halt at Causey Arch, which we shall reach soon.

3. At the top of the steps, turn right and walk parallel to the railway. Keep going until you reach Causey Arch itself on your right. The railway halt is on your left.

There are no station buildings at the halt, but there are two old goods trucks parked in a siding. More historic still is a replica wooden waggon.

☺ This is a replica of one of the wooden waggons which used to cross Causey Arch over 250 years ago, taking coal from the colliery at Tanfield to the River Tyne, where it was loaded onto ships and taken as far as London. It wasn't just the waggons that were wooden – the rails were, too! They used to lay two sets at once so that when the top ones wore through, the waggons could run on the lower pair.

The noticeboard opposite places the events at Tanfield and Causey Arch into the context of a time-line, as well as displaying a pictorial representation of the journey of coal from Tanfield to London via Newcastle.

4. For the moment, resist the temptation to cross the Arch and follow the path a little further to the viewpoint. This is a good photo opportunity. Another information board gives more details of the Arch's history.

Q: How high is the Arch above the Causey Burn stream below?
A: 85ft

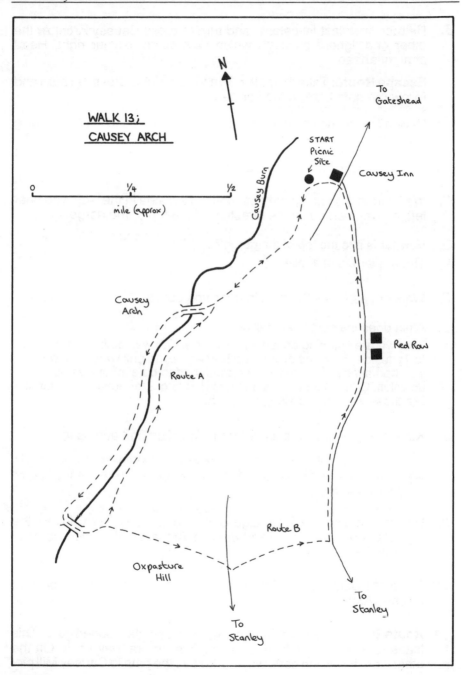

5. Retrace your last few steps, and turn to cross Causey Arch. At the other end, ignore the path which dips down to your right. Head straight ahead.

Escape Route: Take the path down to your right. Cross the burn and follow the path back to the car park.

☺ Have a look at the information board here. There used to be a building here – the evidence of the old stones tells us that, and, according to the information, it was a tollbooth where the people who operated the waggons had to pay to cross Causey Arch.

6. Walk straight on along the path until, at a divide in the way, you bear left, as waymarked, in the direction of the top of the gorge.

Q: How far is it to the top of the gorge?

A: Three-quarters of a mile

7. Walk on, as far as the next information board.

Q: What does the next board tell us?

A: That we are standing on a waggonway, which was built to carry coal to Tyneside, $5\frac{1}{2}$ miles away. The horses had to pull waggons which weighed almost 4 tonnes, so the track had to be almost level, or downhill. Consequently, the builders had to cut terraces and cuttings like those we can see along this path.

8. Keep going until you reach a footbridge. Turn left across it.

You may care to walk on a little before crossing the footbridge, in order to take advantage of a view of East Tanfield Station where steam engines may be seen on operating days.

9. Having crossed the footbridge over the Causey Burn, follow the sharp left bend of the path and walk on. At the top of the rise, come to a T-junction.

10. Route A: Bear left and follow the path through the gorge, back to Causey Arch.

11. Route B: Follow the waymarking right to a single wooden gate. This leads to a pedestrian level crossing over the railway track. On the other side, follow the path, waymarked as the path to Causey Mill picnic site. Cross the stile and continue along the side of a field—up and over the crest.

☺ The field here is very large because the hedgerows have been removed to allow the farmer to use large farm machinery to work the land. So we have moved from a historic landscape of the past to a very modern one. In the distance there are some modern factories now—where once there would have been coal mines and coke ovens.

12. At the skyline is a further stile to cross. Descend to the main road beyond and cross, with care. Follow the signposted public footpath directly opposite. At the bottom of the steps, follow the waymarking to the right before turning left across a waymarked stile. Walk ahead, with a holly hedge to your left. Reaching a new stile, follow the waymark arrow left, down the dip to another arrow at the end of a stone wall. This directs you right. Follow the path down into the valley to cross the footbridge to Causey Mill picnic site.

You may think about taking a rest here before continuing, but be aware of the imminent pub alternative.

13. Walk straight ahead from the footbridge, up the rise and on as far as a stile to cross on to a metalled lane. Bear left along the lane.

☺ This is Beamishburn Road. It is not very busy, but there is some traffic, so be careful.

To the right along here is the Black Horse public house – an alternative refreshment point perhaps.

14. Directly opposite the pub is a wooden stile. Cross it and follow the waymarked footpath hard right along the edge of the pasture. Cross into the succeeding field and then climb over the next waymarked stile, back on to Beamishburn Road. Head left along the lane, as far as the Causey Arch Inn.

Escape routes: There are a couple of waymarked public footpaths on your left which you can use as short cuts back to the Causey Arch car park.

☺ Keep looking on the right for the old Causey School.

Q: What year does it date from?
A: 1896.

15. Turn left at the Causey Arch Inn, down to the main road. Cross and walk down the lane to the level crossing and Causey Arch picnic area beyond.

Wooden waggon, Causey Arch

Other Places of Interest in the Area

Tanfield Railway

The Tanfield Railway is a volunteer-run, restored steam railway. Passenger trains are operated on Sundays and bank holidays between about 11am and 4 pm, and on Thursdays and Saturdays during the school summer holidays. They ply the few miles of track from Marley Hill to East Tanfield, via Causey Arch, and a ride in one of their old wooden carriages is a potential highlight of your day out. To combine such a trip with your walk, an option would be to take the train from Causey Arch to Andrew's House station, where there is a shop and café, as well as an engine shed to visit, before returning to the halt at the Arch. You may need to plan this quite carefully. Enquiries are on (0191) 2742002.

Beamish Museum

Beamish is a re-creation of life in the North of England at the turn of the century. There are live characters providing demonstrations in role. Highlights include the tramway, drift mine, old Board School, with traditional playground games, and farm with animals. Beamish opens daily in summer, but is closed Mondays and Fridays in winter. For information contact the museum on 01207 231811, or access its website on the Internet (http://www.merlins.demon.co.uk/beamish). To reach Beamish from Causey Arch, head first in the direction of Stanley, and then towards Chester-le-Street along the A693.

14. BLANCHLAND

The heart of this pretty village is the enclosed square of tiny stone cottages entered from the north by the side of a stone arch. To the south, the old stone bridge straddles the River Derwent to County Durham. Beside the stone arch is the village post office. This, with its flagged floor and traditional wooden counters, is a real throwback to Victorian times.

The walk begins in Blanchland village (on the B6306 Hexham to Carterway Heads road) and takes in a riverside outward leg followed by a return through coniferous forest.

Starting Point:	Car park, Blanchland village (Grid ref. NY 965504)
Distance:	2½ miles
Terrain:	Most of the walk is on unsurfaced paths, either by the river or in quite dense woodland.
Map:	OS Pathfinder 560 Allendale Town and Blanchland
Public Toilets:	Blanchland
Refreshments:	Blanchland village, including the Lord Crewe Arms and the White Monk tearooms.
Pushchairs:	The section from the village to the Derwent via the Escape Route and back is suitable.

☞ You should pass most of these. See how many you can spot:

☐ drystone wall

☐ ferns

☐ blackberry bushes

☐ black-faced sheep

☐ an oak leaf

☐ a tree stump

☐ a pine cone

☐ a hen house

☐ an old-fashioned telephone box

☐ a Victorian postbox

Blanchland

1. Start from the free car park in Blanchland village. Walk out of the entrance and turn right to walk to the square in the centre of the village, passing through the stone arch there.

2. Walk through the square and on as far as the bridge over the River Derwent, but do not cross it. Instead turn left to join the riverside path which is accessed by turning hard right alongside the parapet until you come to the river bank itself. Turn left to walk along in the same direction as the Derwent is flowing.

Q: Where does the waymark sign say we are heading to?
A: Carrick, 1¾ miles

☺ As we walk along here, look out for wire cages on the banks. These are grabions. The stones inside them are to protect the riverbank from being worn away or eroded by the river current. They are on the outside of river bends because this is where the force of the river is greater.

3. Keep going along the riverside path. On encountering a pair of ladder stiles, cross them both and keep walking by the river, crossing a broad area of grassland on the inside of a meander.

☺ Run ahead to the waymark post and see what it can tell us.

Blanchland is 1 mile behind you. Straight ahead is Carrick Picnic Site (1 mile), and to the left Blanchland ¾ is indicated along the public bridleway.

You now have two routes from which to choose.
First, the directions for **Route A:**

4. Turn left along the drystone-walled track and keep straight ahead until there is a right-angled corner taking you leftward.

☺ This flat area we are now crossing is the flood plain of the river. The land here would be wetter if it were not for the land drains we can see dug in the soil next to the path.

For **Route B** follow the following directions.

5. At the waymark post, carry straight ahead and walk the mile to the riverside picnic site at Carrick, retracing your steps back to this point to rejoin Route A.

Alternatively, you could visit the picnic site by car after your walk or even park the car there at the outset and use Route B as the beginning and end of your walk.

6. On Route A, turn the right-angled corner and walk on as far as the road.

Escape Route: You could turn left and walk alongside the road back to the village.

7. Turn right and walk uphill.

☺ Look out on the left for a really old, gnarled tree.

Q: What species of tree is it?
A: Oak

8. Keep alongside the road until you enter the wood. Look out for a public footpath waymarker on your left. Turn left, almost back on yourselves, to approach a waymarked seven-bar gate. Pass through and walk along the woodland track to a divide. Bear right.

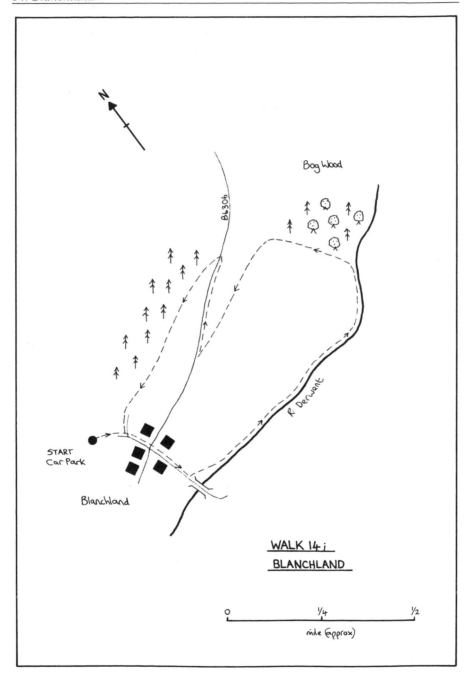

N

Bog Wood

B6306

R. Derwent

START
Car Park

Blanchland

WALK 14 i
BLANCHLAND

0   ¼   ½

mile (approx)

This woodland section provides a welcome opportunity for children to run ahead and feel they are explorers – provided they stick to the path of course.

9. As the woods clear, a track joins from the right. Continue straight ahead along the grassy track. If you have reached a rightward bend in the track you have gone too far. Opposite the path you want is a small gate set in the fence to your right.

Start to look out for a waymark post on your left. It may be a good idea to enlist the children's help in this.

10. Turn left at the post. Walk downhill along the narrower path, which has taken you away from the main track.

☺ This part of the path has lots of pine needles. These needles are the leaves of the trees which have fallen to the ground as litter. Coniferous trees (those with cones) have needle-like leaves to help them keep moisture during dry periods of winter. This works because the needle leaves have a smaller surface area to lose water from.

11. Reaching a clearer area, where a way appears to join you from the left, walk straight ahead and keep going until you reach a point where there are tracks going to the right and to the left. Turn left and down.

Waymarking here may tempt you to the right. Ignore it.

12. Emerge from the woods at the back of a row of cottages. Bear right down the lane to emerge opposite the car park in Blanchland.

Other Places of Interest in the Area

Derwent Reservoir

East of Blanchland is the Derwent Reservoir. There are designated picnic sites here, offering the children the chance to run about. On the north shore, there is also a nature reserve.

Edmundbyers

At the opposite end of the Derwent Reservoir is the pretty village of Edmundbyers. There is a village pub here – an alternative refreshment opportunity to the Lord Crewe Arms in Blanchland, which is more of a hotel.

Hexham

The market town of Hexham is quite nearby (8 miles to the north). Saturday is a good day to visit for a bit of country town bustle. There is a small market and numerous shops from chic little boutiques and delicatessens to Robbs department store. Midweek, the market is held on Tuesdays. The abbey dates from the 12th century, but there is an older, Saxon crypt.

15. DURHAM CITY

The historic cathedral city of Durham is the backdrop for this short, but intricate walk from the bustling Market Place, through the medieval streets and Norman cathedral to the tranquil College square and dramatic, wooded river banks. The walk provides a tour of the city on foot, and can easily be turned into a full day by touring the cathedral, and maybe the castle, more extensively, and taking advantage of the riverside leisure opportunities – including the famous Browns' boats for hire from Elvet Bridge and the more recent pleasure boat passenger trips.

Starting Point:	The Market Place (Grid ref. NZ 276425)
Distance:	2 miles
Terrain:	A mixture of pavements and unsurfaced, riverbank, woodland paths. There is a steep flight of steps at Kingsgate Bridge.
Map:	OS Pathfinder 572 Durham
Public Toilets:	In the city centre, and at the cathedral
Refreshments:	In the city centre, and at the cathedral
Pushchairs:	Most of the walk could be completed with a pushchair. However, the steps at the cathedral end of Kingsgate Bridge are certainly an obstacle. To avoid these, choose either of the first two Escape Routes.

☞ You should pass most of these. See how many you can spot:

☐ Three cathedral towers

☐ a window shaped like a rose

☐ a shield on a wall

☐ someone fishing

☐ a boat landing

☐ a green dome

☐ a rowing crew

☐ a city crest (a red cross on a black background)

☐ a duck

☐ a bicycle-riding rowing coach

1. Start from the Market Place, at the two statues.

☺ The statues here are of Neptune with his trident and of the 3rd Marquis of Londonderry on his horse. The Marquis used to be an important coal-owner in the area around Durham. That means he used to own a lot of the coalmines for which Durham used to be famous. Look in the horse's mouth. What is missing?

There is no tongue. It is said that the realisation of this flaw in his other-wise perfect statue caused the sculptor to take his own life.

2. Orientate yourselves so that St Nicholas's Church is behind you. Take the slightly leftward road – Saddler Street – out of the Market Place and walk up to the fork. Bear right into the street known as the Bailey. Walk up to the next fork and bear right along Owengate to the Palace Green.

Arriving at Palace Green, look for a frieze on the facing wall of the Cathedral, near the Rose Window end, which depicts the Dun Cow Legend. Indicate it.

☺ There is a legend about how the cathedral came to be built here. Monks from the Abbey at Lindisfarne were transporting St Cuthbert's body,

Durham cathedral

looking for a final resting-place for the saint. They met a woman with a dun cow who pointed out this site. When they wheeled their cart over to it, its wheels jammed. The monks took this to be a sign that they had found the spot to bury Cuthbert, and so they did. The present cathedral was built on the site by the Normans, and had its 900th birthday in 1993.

3. Continue straight ahead, the cathedral to your left.

☺ Over to the right we can see the bastion of Durham Castle. It and the cathedral were built on a steep, rocky peninsula, nearly surrounded by the River Wear, because it was an easily defended site. The main danger was regular raiding of the North of England by the Scots. Nowadays, the castle is used as Durham University College.

4. Enter the cathedral via the main door with the Sanctuary Knocker.

☺ This lion's head knocker is the Sanctuary Knocker. Hundreds of years ago, people running away from the law could claim safety, or sanctuary, in the cathedral by knocking. The forces of the Crown were not allowed to enter the cathedral, so the fugitive would be safe – while inside the cathedral, at least!

5. Inside the cathedral, walk across the main aisle to the glazed wooden doors. Pass through into the cloisters.

Clearly, you may want to take time out to explore the cathedral. You will find the information desk as you enter the building.

6. You enter the cloisters at the diagonally opposite corner from your exit. So, pick your route, and walk along two sides of the square to that opposite corner, where a tunnel leads you through to the open square known as the College.

Immediately on your right is the small memorial garden of the Durham Light Infantry (DLI). Around the square, the coats of arms of various Prince Bishops of Durham are mounted. There is a framed key in the arch round the corner to your left. Children may enjoy spotting some of these shields. The College is a pleasantly quiet square to while away a few minutes before continuing.

7. Exit the College via the tunnel which is to your right when you first enter from the cathedral.

The gate here is open until at least 6pm – later in the summer (until 10pm in June). Pause at the top of the path beyond the tunnel.

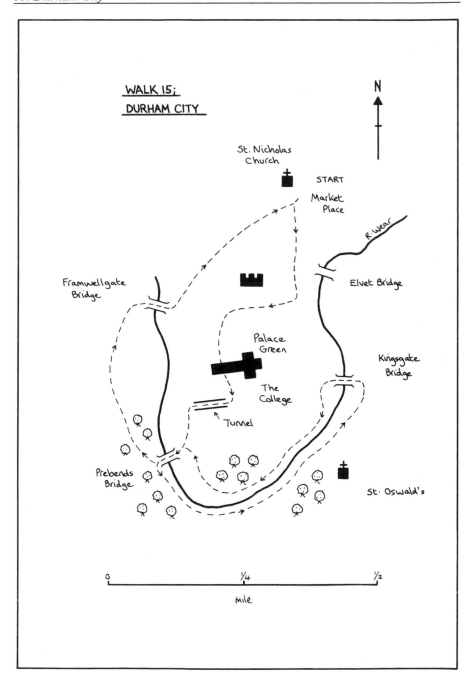

WALK 15;
DURHAM CITY

N

St. Nicholas
Church

START

Market
Place

R. Wear

Framwellgate
Bridge

Elvet Bridge

Palace
Green

Kingsgate
Bridge

The
College

Tunnel

Prebends
Bridge

St. Oswald's

0   ¼   ½

Mile

☺ Looking over the wall, you can see a weir on the Wear! Next to it is a building that used to be a mill.

8. Turn left down the ramp. Keep going straight down to Prebends Bridge. Turn right and cross the bridge.

Escape Route 1: Turn left through the arch and walk down the Bailey to the Market Place, via the end of the cobbled lane to Kingsgate Bridge.

☺ At the end of the bridge is a plaque with a poem. Go ahead and see who wrote the verse.

It was Sir Walter Scott.

9. Having crossed the bridge, turn left.

Escape Route 2: Turn right instead. You are now picking up the end of this walk, so follow the last few directions to the Market Place.

10. On the main route, follow the lower riverbank path around the outer bank of the meander.

☺ The river is in quite a steep gorge here. This is called an incised meander. After the Ice Age, the land sprang back up from the relief of having the weight of ice removed. The River Wear was able to cut into this so that its bend, or meander, became steeply incised (cut) into the rock.

The last advance of the ice was at its greatest extent approximately 18 000 years ago. However, the ice has advanced and retreated over Britain on numerous occasions (up to 20 in the last 2 million years), so it does not follow that the Wear's meander was incised in such a short period as 18 000 years.

11. As you round the meander, the path will lead you up towards the tower of St Oswald's Church. Keep to it, ignoring minor distractions – particularly to the right, and walk through the churchyard to the war memorial cross.

☺ On the left of the cross is a rosemary bush. Have a smell!

12. Keep walking and you will join Church Street. Follow the pavement downhill a little to round the bend. Turn left here, next to the concrete Dunelm House (Durham Students Union, DSU) to cross Kingsgate Bridge.

☺ Looking ahead to the cathedral from here we can see a large, round, stained glass window called the Rose Window. Each of the petals is a pane depicting one of the apostles.

Concrete Kingsgate Bridge dates from 1963. Its construction was in two separate halves – each initially parallel to the river -which were then swung round to meet. Halfway across you can spot the join!

Escape Route 3: At the end of the bridge, climb the 17 steps and walk the length of the cobbled street ahead. Turn right and make your way down the Bailey to the Market Place.

13. For the main route, turn left at the end of the bridge, and descend the long flight of steps to the riverside.

Q: How many steps are there?
A: 103

14. Turn right at the bottom and follow the towpath right round the inner bank of the meander, past the colonnaded ruin of Count's House to a fork. Bear right and pass the tree sculpture on your left. Continue until you reach and re-cross Prebends Bridge. This time, turn right at the end and take the upper (left-hand) riverbank path from the obelisk.

Along here are classic views of Durham Cathedral.

15. The path leads you to a metalled lane. Turn right and follow this lane down to a junction just past the City Library. Turn right and right again to cross Framwellgate Bridge. Walk up Silver Street to the Market Place.

Other Places of Interest in the Area

Finchale Abbey

A possible picnic site away from the city is the riverside ruined priory at Finchale. Follow the A691/ Ai77 Consett road out of the city centre. Head towards Framwellgate Moor and take the signposted minor road from there, turning right at the Salutation pub, via Newton Hall. Always open.

DLI Museum and Arts Centre

Just outside of the city centre, alongside the A691 Consett road, and well-signposted, this museum houses military paraphernalia and equipment from the history of Durham's distinguished county regiment. Open Tuesdays to Saturdays 10am to 5pm and Sundays from 2pm. Telephone 0191 3842214.

Botanic Garden, Durham University

Also well signposted from the city centre, this nature-lovers' attraction is off the South Road (A1050 towards Darlington). It is an 18-acre garden including exotic trees from the Himalayas and tropical and cactus houses. There is a visitor centre and toilets. Open daily from April to October (10am to 5pm). Telephone (0191) 3742671.

16. WESTGATE IN WEARDALE

Westgate is situated in Weardale, 6 miles west of Stanhope. The Weardale Way passes through the village and most of this walk is along a loop of that long-distance path, taking in the valley of Middlehope Burn. This is rich in remains of the former lead mining industry which once flourished in Weardale.

The start of the walk is behind the restored Westgate-in-Weardale railway station; the picnic tables are to the front overlooking the river. The station was opened in 1895 when the Wear Valley line was extended from Stanhope to Wearhead. It carried passengers up and down the dale for over 50 years.

Starting Point:	Old Westgate Station picnic site car park (Grid ref. NY 911381)
Distance:	4 miles
Terrain:	Mostly unsurfaced paths, no especially steep sections.
Map:	OS Outdoor Leisure 31, Teesdale
Toilets:	Hare and Hounds pub in Westgate (for customers); the Dales Centre in Stanhope
Refreshments:	Hare and Hounds, Westgate – beer garden
Pushchairs:	Apart from the village and environs, and possibly the section of the Weardale Way as far as High Mill, this is not a walk suited to pushchairs

☞ You should pass most of these. See how many you can spot:

☐ a wind vane shaped like a locomotive

☐ drystone walls

☐ a children's playground

☐ caravans

☐ a memorial clock

☐ a small waterfall

☐ an old mine

☐ a sheep with a red mark

☐ a ford

☐ an abandoned farmhouse

1. Start by walking out of the car park exit and turning right along the lane to cross the bridge over the river into the village.

☺ The river here is the Wear.

Q: How many arches does the bridge have?

A: 3

☺ Westgate gained its name by being the gate to the west of a deer park for the medieval bishops of Durham to go hunting. Further down Weardale, on the way to Stanhope, is Eastgate.

2. Turn left along the village street, crossing the road when safe. Turn right in the direction of Rookhope, as signposted. Continue until faced by a row of cottages with semi-circular windows above their doors. Bear left onto the waymarked, unsurfaced lane.

☺ This is the start of the section of the Weardale Way we will be following today. This path goes from Wearhead all the way down river to Sunderland.

Q: How far is it to Middleton Mine?

A: 1 mile (on waymark sign).

☺ We will be passing Middleton Mine's ruins along the way. Along this walk we will see the remains of all sorts of old mining buildings. Weardale used to be an important lead mining area.

3. Follow the lane to a gate at High Mill. Keep to the path to reach and pass through a second gate. Continue until you cross a waymarked footbridge, the first of two.

This wooded section of the walk lends itself to suggesting to the children that they are out exploring. Providing they stick to the path, it might be an idea to allow them to run on and seek out the way.

4. When you reach a single white gate in front of some ruins, pass through it and walk past the ruins on your right.

☺ These ruins are old mining structures. Remember we said that Weardale used to have a major lead mining industry. Look out for a place where the stream has been diverted underground.

5. Passing the main ruins, bear right and continue to where the stream

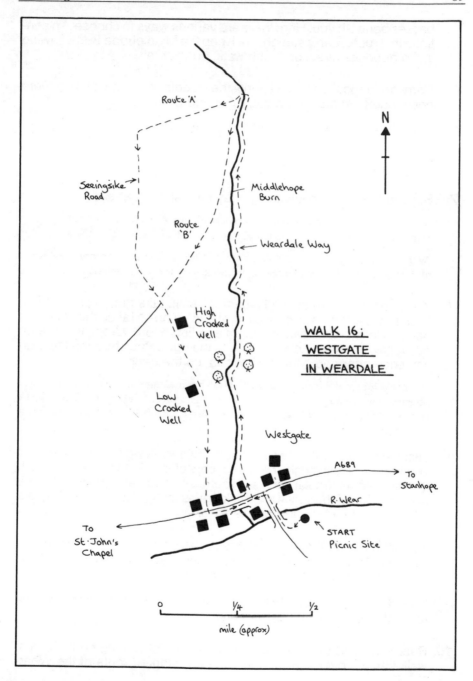

Route 'A'

Seeingsike Road

Middlehope Burn

Route 'B'

Weardale Way

N

High Crooked Well

Low Crooked Well

WALK 16;
WESTGATE
IN WEARDALE

Westgate

A689

To Stanhope

R. Wear

To St. John's Chapel

START Picnic Site

0   ¼   ½

mile (approx)

passes beneath you. Here there are various ways to choose. To continue this route, carry straight on. Keep the Middlehope Burn, flowing in the opposite direction to the walk, on your left.

6. Carry on, negotiating a stile, until the woodland gives way to a more open moorland scrub and you reach more ruins.

☺ These are the remains of Middleton Mine itself.

Clearly children are likely to want to explore. Some care will be needed – this is not a prepared heritage site.

7. Beyond the mine, follow the grassy path straight ahead.

Look out on the right for the stone-arched entrance of a former mine tunnel. Indicate this if you spot it. You could walk up to it and peer in.

As you continue you will see a stile on the other bank of the stream. This is not part of your route. Stick to the bank you are on for the moment.

8. Keep going. Where the path seems to split, take the grassier fork to keep the drystone wall on your right and go on as far as the waymark post. Turn left down to the stream and find a ford. Cross the stream and follow the track up and round to the right. Pass through the gate you encounter and continue beyond, up the track.

You could instead decide to follow the footpath alongside this far bank of the stream. It will bring you to the point where the track of Seeingsike Road meets the end of the metalled road. This alternative, Route B, is about a quarter of a mile shorter.

☺ There are impressive views from here. To our left we can see down into Weardale and to the right the open moors of the North Pennines, which is described as 'England's last wilderness'. You can see why. On the opposite side of the valley is a track just as straight as this, leading to a T-junction with a lane, just as this does.

9. To continue with the longer Route A, walk on until you come to a T-junction. Turn left along the unsurfaced track of Seeingsike Road and walk on until you round a steep depression.

☺ Look down in the steep hollow. At the bottom there are some stones round the entrance of a disused mine shaft.

10. Reach the end of a metalled road. Instead of turning right along it, walk straight over, leaving the main waymarked route of the Wear-

Waterfall on Middlehope Burn

dale Way, and pass through the gate to walk straight on. Pass through the next gate and continue past a stone-built house on your left. After negotiating a third gate, reach the gated entrance of Low Crooked Well on your right.

☺ This big house is called Low Crooked Well. Look at the lions on the gateposts. Soon we will be able to see Westgate village again. Keep a look out for it.

11. Follow the now grassy track down to the next gate. Keep going, beyond a copse of trees you will reach. Carry on down to, and then through, a farmyard, before following the ensuing lane to the road. Turn left along the street of Westgate village until you reach the Hare and Hounds, then turn right to walk back to the car park.

Other Places of Interest in the Area

Dales Centre, Stanhope

About a 6 mile drive to the east down Weardale is the small town of Stanhope. The Dales Centre there includes craft workshops.

Killhope Wheel Lead Mining Centre

Park Level Mine at Killhope recreates the working conditions of the lead miners of the late 19th century. Guided tours are available. Warm clothing and waterproof footwear (wellies) are recommended, even in summer. The giant turning waterwheel is the biggest in the North of England. There is a visitor centre with exhibition, café and gift shop. The centre is open from April to October and in November on Sundays only. The telephone number is (01388) 537505.

Weardale Leisure Complex, Eastgate

Between Westgate and Stanhope, this indoor attraction may be worth investigating.

17. CASTLE EDEN

Castle Eden Dene is one of several steep-sided, wooded gorges along the East Durham coast. Like the others, it is the result of more energetic erosion by rivers following the end of the last Ice Age, when the relative fall in sea level, compared to the land which was rising as it sprang back from being pushed down by the weight of the ice, increased the gradient of coastal streams, giving them increased ability to cut into the land.

Castle Eden Dene is now partly a nature reserve. It is densely wooded and this walk should appeal to the explorer inside the curious child. Narrow paths snake among the trees, up and down the steep sides of the Dene and alongside Castle Eden Burn.

Starting Point:	Castle Eden church (Grid ref. NZ 428385)
Distance:	2 miles or 3½ miles
Terrain:	Mostly unsurfaced woodland paths, which can be slippery in wet weather.
Map:	OS Pathfinder 582 Hartlepool
Refreshments:	The Castle Eden Inn
Pushchairs:	Only the wider section from the church straight down to the burn is really suitable (about half a mile each way).

☞ You should pass most of these. See how many you can spot:

☐   a beech tree

☐   a sycamore

☐   a fallen tree

☐   blackberry bushes

☐   a rhododendron bush

☐   holly

☐   ferns

☐   roschips

☐   an English Nature oak tree symbol

☐   a painted red squirrel, or even a real one!

Castle Eden, in The Dene

1. Start at the church. Walk down the lane to the castle gates and pass through the single metal gate to their right. Begin to walk along the drive but turn right again down to green metal gates. Enter the Castle Eden Nature Reserve and walk downhill.

☺ Castle Eden Dene is a nature reserve. That means that the plants and animals in the woods are protected and looked after. Denes are very steep valleys. The streams in the reserve now, like the one on our right, are far too small to have cut the dene into the rock. In the past, at the end of the last Ice Age, they would have been much bigger because of the melted ice, and sufficiently powerful to erode the rock to make such steep-sided valleys.

2. As you descend you will pass a point where two denes intersect on your right. Just beyond this you are faced with a choice of routes. For the shorter walk (Route A), continue straight ahead.

    Route B is an extension loop of about 1½ miles which will return you to this point.

3. **To begin Route B**, turn right and walk uphill, swinging right at the top of the rise. Where there is a fork, bear right and walk along.

Along here you are on the edge of the nature reserve. Over to the right is a large field from which hedgerows have clearly been removed. This common alteration to the landscape is, of course, controversial. Loss of habitat and scenic value are pitted against economic benefits of maximising the use of the land and of large farming machinery. Perhaps you could discuss this issue with the children.

4. Keep following the track back into and then out of the woods until you encounter an English Nature signboard low to your left. Turn left and follow the path down, initially almost back on yourself.

In looking out for this sign, you should be alerted by the return of field over to your right, with a plantation beyond.

5. Follow the winding path, in all its twists and turns, for its full length.

☺ This is really like exploring – like being in the middle of a jungle.

6. After some time, you emerge at the fork you met earlier. Bear right, down the track to the crossroads of tracks where Route B began, and this time turn right to join Route A again.

Escape route: Turn left to return to your car.

7. To follow Route A, walk downhill, sweeping right, until you come to a T-junction of ways. Bear right and walk down to cross the bridge over Castle Eden Burn.

☺ Burn is a north country dialect word for a stream. Beck is another.

8. As soon as you have crossed the bridge, turn sharp left to follow the path along the burn-side until you come to a footbridge over the stream.

Indicate the cliff to your right. Ivy and other plants trail impressively down the face of the sands.

9. Walk on, around a meander, and continue to a quite steeply rising section – up and over some steps. Keep going until a path meets you from higher on your left.

Look down to the right here and you will see the burn take a distinct loop around a rocky obstacle.

10. Turn left, up this path.

At the top of the rise is a large beech tree. Standing beside this affords a dramatic view into the dene below, but children will need to be warned not to be too close to the precipitous edge.

11. Coming to a section of broader track, turn left by a red squirrel waymark post.

☺ Look at the seat here. It is made from a tree trunk.

12. Approaching a gate to the grounds of the now empty large house of Castle Eden itself, turn left just in front of it. Walk downhill until you reach, again, the divide in the ways where Routes A and B diverge. This time turn right to retrace your steps back to the car. This entails bearing right again at the second fork.

☺ The woods we have walked through today are what is called 'ancient woodland'. This means that they are part of the original wild woods that covered most of England after the Ice Age, before people cleared most of them to make space for farming and for settlements. Steep places like this were difficult to work so they were often left alone.

Other Places of Interest in the Area

Crimdon Dene

A further dene to the south, Crimdon Dene emerges on to a sand dune coast. There is a beach here. Crimdon can be reached by driving along the A1068 Blackhall to Hartlepool road. Turn left to Blackhall at the end of the lane from Castle Eden church.

Hartlepool Historic Quay

This is a recreation of an 18th-century harbour such as the one that would then have existed at Hartlepool. The quay is ringed by exhibits and activities, including a vivid reconstruction of a naval sailing ship under attack and Skittle Square – an 18th-century children's playground. The historic quay is open daily from 10am to 5pm. There is an information line – tel. 01429 860006.

Durham City

The historic city of Durham with its cathedral and castle (see Walk 15) is only about 10 miles to the west. Follow the A181.

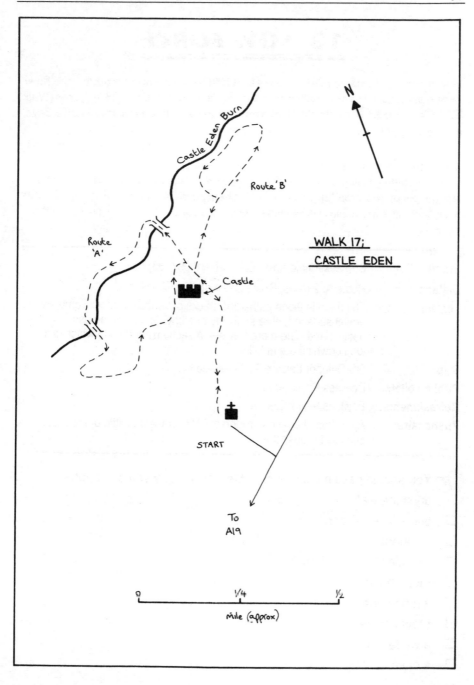

Castle Eden Burn

Route 'B'

N

Route 'A'

WALK 17;
CASTLE EDEN

Castle

START

To
A19

0   ¼   ½
mile (approx)

18. LOW FORCE

Low Force, as its name might suggest, is a little way downstream on the River Tees — about a mile and a half — from the perhaps better-known High Force (Walk 19). It is, however, a very pretty sight and, coupled with the fall at Gibson's Cave, makes this walk something of a waterfalls experience.

The walk begins at the Bowlees Picnic Area, which is signposted off the B6277, about 3 miles or so west of Middleton-in-Teesdale. At Bowlees there is a Visitor Centre housing exhibitions of local geology and natural history, and showing how the people of the area have adapted to their physical surroundings. In the car park there is a drystone wall exhibit to which visitors are welcome to add further stones.

Starting Point:	Bowlees Picnic Area (Grid ref. NY 907283)
Distance:	Route A: 2 miles, Route B: an additional half mile.
Terrain:	The route is along paths and tracks of various grades. Some are gravel-surfaced, others muddy or stony, and some across pastureland. There are few steep sections, and none which last long or which are uphill.
Map:	OS Outdoor Leisure 31 Teesdale
Public Toilets:	Bowlees Picnic Area
Refreshments:	Bowlees Visitor Centre
Pushchairs:	Apart from the lanes around the Visitor Centre, little of the route is suitable for pushchairs.

☞ You should pass most of these. See how many you can spot:

☐ drystone wall

☐ black-faced sheep

☐ a waterfall

☐ potholes in a river bed

☐ rabbit holes

☐ a pine cone

☐ brown cattle

☐ a white farm

☐ a cave

1. Start from the picnic area car park. Cross the footbridge and continue, as signposted to the Visitor Centre.

Q: What date is on the Visitor Centre out-house?
A: 1868.

☺ Look for the sensory garden where there are plants chosen for their appeal to each of the five senses. Thistle is for touch.

Q: Which plants are for smell and taste?
A: Lavender and mint.

2. Walk along the path to the left of the Visitor Centre and emerge through a single wooden gate. Walk on, to the right of a row of whitewashed cottages, as far as the road.

Q: The Visitor Centre is a converted church. How long ago was it built?
A: The current year minus 1904.

☺ Cottages which are white like these can be found all over Teesdale. It means they belong to the estate of Lord Barnard. Barnard Castle is a ruined castle in the market town of the same name a few miles downstream from here.

3. Carefully cross the road and pass through the kissing gate opposite which is signposted to the Wynch Bridge (300 metres). Keep following the path beyond a second kissing gate and through a narrow, gap-style stone stile, to descend into woodland.

The path will take you directly to the Wynch Bridge. However, views of the Low Force waterfall are to be gained by veering over to the right before you reach the lifebelt.

4. Cross the Wynch Bridge.

☺ There is a viewing area over to the right when we have crossed the bridge. The rock that has made the waterfall is part of the Whin Sill. This is a band of igneous rock – that means made from molten magma which has solidified – that lies underneath much of Northumbria and comes to the surface in a variety of places including High Force. Because the rock is resistant (difficult to wear away), it often forms cliffs which people have used for castles, like Bamburgh, or along which to to build sections of the Roman Wall.

The Whin Sill is composed of quartz dolerite rock. A feature is the jointing, or cracking, of the rock into hexagonal columns (similar to the Giant's Causeway) which are evident here and which you may like to point out.

Low Force

☺ The Tees has made the waterfall by wearing away the rock of its channel. Because some parts are harder to wear away (more resistant) they stick up as steps. This starts the waterfall's formation.

As waterfalls develop, the water which falls over the step undercuts it. In time, the step collapses and the whole fall has, as a result, moved back, or retreated. This leaves a gorge. Such a gorge is visible on your left as you cross the Wynch Bridge.

5. From the end of the bridge, turn hard left along the riverside path which initially climbs over a few stones.

Be careful not to go through a single wooden gate leading into a field. This may appear tempting, but is the wrong way!

☺ In the rock beside the stream there are round potholes. The Tees has made these. When there is a lot of water, such as after a storm or the melting of winter snow, the river picks up stones and swirls them around. They drill into the rock floor to form these potholes.

6. Keep going along the riverside path, crossing a small footbridge over a tributary stream, and continuing without deviation until you reach a

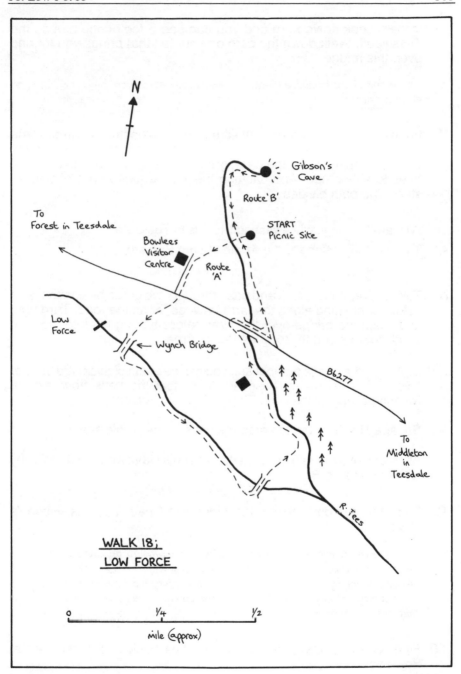

N

Gibson's Cave

Route 'B'

To Forest in Teesdale

Bowlees Visitor Centre

Route 'A'

START Picnic Site

Low Force

Wynch Bridge

B6277

To Middleton in Teesdale

R. Tees

WALK 18;
LOW FORCE

0   ¼   ½

mile (approx)

lifebelt. Look down here and you can see a footbridge across the Tees itself. Walk down the path on your left that brings you to, and over, this bridge.

At the end of the bridge, a flight of steep, stone steps very suddenly appears, so take care.

7. From the bridge, head straight across the cow pasture towards some minor farm buildings, passing through the gateway just to their right. Bear left and make for the wide, green space between high banks of trees to either side. Approaching the whitewashed barn of a farmstead, the path divides.

Q: Why are buildings whitewashed like this in Teesdale?

A: To show they belong to the estate of Lord Barnard.

8. Take the right-hand fork and pass through two gates beside the farm before continuing along the farm track as far as the road. Turn right and cross the bridge over the river before turning left into the lane which returns you to Bowlees Picnic Area.

☺ Look over the bridge parapet and you can see nets of thick wire used to hold stones in place. These are to protect the bank from erosion (wearing away) by the river. They are called grabions.

Escape Route: You can stop the walk at the picnic site.

Alternatively, you can continue to Gibson's Cave and its waterfall by following **Route B:**

9. From the car park, follow the signposted path towards Gibson's Cave.

Along the way there is a minor waterfall with a viewpoint, and also a footbridge over the river which you should not cross if you intend to reach the cave itself. As you continue you will pass through a gate on which a notice warns that this is not a right of way and walkers continue to the cave at their own risk – not that of Lord Barnard.

10. From Gibson's Cave, retrace your steps back to the car park at Bowlees.

Other Places of Interest in the Area

Barnard Castle

The ruins of the twelfth-century castle dominate the still narrow bridge across the Tees which connects County Durham to North Yorkshire. Barnard Castle today is a lively market town (market day is Wednesday) with plenty of cafés and inns. On the road out towards Whorlton – where there is a lido – is Bowes Museum, where collections of art and furniture are housed in a grand house.

Middleton-in-Teesdale

The smaller dales town of Middleton lies between Low Force and 'Barney'. There are a few shops and pubs serving food. It is possible to get down to the riverside by the bridge in order to to stroll or spin stones into the clear water.

High Force

High Force is England's highest waterfall and is a spectacle not to miss on a visit to Teesdale. To approach the falls on the south bank entails a proper walk (see Walk 19), but there is an easier, more touristy access on the north bank. This starts from the High Force Hotel which stands alongside the B6277, 2 miles west of Bowlees. There is a car park and a pay-to-enter path down to the falls.

19. HOLWICK AND HIGH FORCE

Holwick is a small hamlet of stone-built cottages and a pub at the end of a 3-mile road to nowhere else. It retains a distinct feel of the wilderness edge. To reach Holwick, drive along the signposted minor road from the opposite side of the Tees from Middleton-in-Teesdale. The Strathmore Arms pub serves food and is open all day.

Both High Force and Low Force are passed by this walk. Low Force (see also Walk 18), the slightly more downstream of the two, is reached first. High Force cascades majestically over the edge of the Whin Sill, whose resistant rock created the initial step from which the Tees carved the fall. Downstream of the fall is a gorge along which the fall has retreated over the millennia as the river has undercut the waterfall face, causing repeated collapse.

On the way to High Force you will be walking through part of the Upper Teesdale Nature Reserve. Managed by English Nature, this is home to many animals including rabbits, which you may well see. There is a unique flora in Upper Teesdale, found where the grainy sugar limestone comes close to the surface.

Starting Point: The Strathmore Arms, Holwick (Grid ref. NY 909268)
Distance: 4 miles
Terrain: Apart from an initial section of metalled lane, most of this route is on country paths, either beside the river or across fields. The stretch inside the nature reserve is gravel-surfaced.
Map: OS Outdoor Leisure 31 Teesdale
Toilets: Strathmore Arms pub (for customers)
Refreshments: Strathmore Arms, Holwick or in Middleton-in-Teesdale
Pushchairs: This is not a pushchair walk.

☞ You should pass most of these. See how many you can spot:
☐ a drystone wall
☐ a Dales Barn
☐ a suspension footbridge
☐ at least three lifebelts
☐ a duck
☐ a rabbit or rabbit hole
☐ an acorn waymark symbol
☐ a gorge
☐ two waterfalls
☐ Whin Sill rock

High Force

1. Start facing the Strathmore Arms and head right, up the valley and past the telephone box, to a road junction. Turn right and walk along to the cattle grid.

☺ Holwick has some cliffs behind it called Holwick Scars. There used to be mining here, but not any more.

Q: How do cattle grids work?
A: The bars stop animals like cattle and sheep crossing the grid because they might catch their feet in the gaps. It saves the trouble of opening and shutting a gate every time people pass.

2. Crossing the cattle grid, bear right, as signed, along the grassy path which crosses the pasture diagonally. Make for the stone gap stile you can see when you are halfway over the field.

☺ The isolated barn we can see here is called a Dales Barn. On the other side of the valley barns and farms are painted white to show that they belong to the estate of Lord Barnard.

3. Head diagonally left to the gap stile in the bottom corner and then continue along the path to emerge, via a single gate, at the Wynch Bridge and Low Force.

Crossing the bridge is not part of the route though children will no doubt want to do so. Low Force can be seen and photographed from the opposite bank, too.

☺ This is Low Force waterfall, so-called because it is further down the Tees, as well as smaller, than High Force which we will see later. Rivers make waterfalls. This is because of differences in the rocks over which they flow. Where one band of rock is more resistant to being worn away by the river, it will tend to form a step, which is the beginning of the waterfall.

4. Follow the waymarked path upstream along the riverside and simply keep going until you reach another footbridge which is gated.

Remember you should still be on the south bank.

☺ We are now at Holwick Head.

Q: Why is there a gate on the bridge?

A: So that sheep do not stray across to the other bank of the river where the land is owned by a different estate.

☺ The land on the southern bank is part of the Strathmore estate. The pub in Holwick is called the Strathmore Arms and its sign shows the coat of arms of the landed family. We will have a look at it at the end of the walk.

Escape Route: Turn left here, go up to the stone house of Holwick Head, and left again through the gate to follow the track to Hield House. Return to Holwick as described later.

5. To continue the route to High Force, walk on, up the cobbled incline, to the gated beginning of the Upper Teesdale Nature Reserve. Enter.

Q: Who runs the Nature Reserve and why are unique flowers found only here?

A: English Nature. There is a special sort of rock, called sugar limestone, which makes the soil very different.

6. Walk on to High Force.

The fall and its gorge are not fenced. Clearly children need to be carefully supervised and kept away from the edge. Just before you reach the gorge the grav-

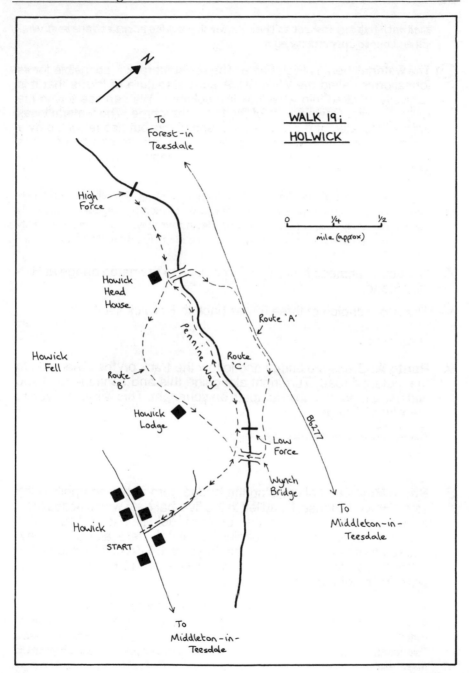

N

To
Forest-in
Teesdale

WALK 19;
HOLWICK

High
Force

0   ¼   ½
mile (approx)

Howick
Head
House

Route 'A'

Howick
Fell

Pennine Way

Route
'C'

Route
'B'

Howick
Lodge

Low
Force

B6277

Wynch
Bridge

Howick

START

To
Middleton-in-
Teesdale

To
Middleton-in-
Teesdale

elled path has an offshoot to the right which provides access to the best viewing and photo opportunity spot.

☺ The waterfall here is High Force. The resistant rock responsible for its
formation is called the Whin Sill. A special feature of this is that it is
vertically cracked into what look like columns. We can see this in the
rock opposite. Downstream of the fall is the gorge. The waterfall was
originally located at the downstream end of this but has retreated over
the millennia as the water cascading down into its plunge pool has
undercut the face of the fall. We can see this happening today at the foot
of High Force.

The vertical lining of the Whin Sill is columnar jointing. The sill was originally
formed deep underground by the solidification of molten magma. As it slowly
cooled and hardened, it cracked in this distinctive way. The columns actually
have a hexagonal section. You may be able to identify and indicate examples.

7. Retrace your steps from High Force back to the gated bridge at Holwick Head.

There is a choice of three routes back to Holwick itself:

8. **Route A:** Cross the bridge and follow the track on the other side to
the metalled road. Turn right alongside this and continue until you
find a waymarked public footpath on your right. This will return you to
the Wynch Bridge.

The road can be quite busy in summer.

9. **Route B:** Instead of crossing the bridge, turn right and uphill to the
stone Holwick House. Head left to the five-bar gate which accesses a
track that will take you past the corner of Hield House and beyond to
the point where metalling begins. Bear left here along the waymarked footpath to emerge a little beyond the Wynch Bridge on the
footpath you followed down from Holwick at the beginning of the
walk. Turn right to complete the route.

The track is a public right of way although it is not waymarked until you have
passed Hield House. Beyond Hield House, the right of way has been altered
slightly, by statutory order, and no longer leads directly to the Wynch Bridge.
This means that it may be slightly different from the path shown on your OS
map. Follow the waymarking.

10. **Route C:** Simply retrace your steps back to the Wynch Bridge. Turn right there, through the single gate, and return to Holwick.

This is not a circular route, but may be preferred by children since it keeps next to the river. In distance, there is little to choose between the three routes.

Other Places of Interest in the Area

Middleton in Teesdale

The nearest shops to Holwick are in Middleton, where there is a choice of refreshment facilities. See Walk 18.

Bowlees Visitor Centre and Gibson's Cave

There is a picnic site and the visitor centre exhibition offers some shelter. For details, again see Walk 18.

Barnard Castle

The principal market town of Teesdale. See Walk 18.

20. ROMALDKIRK

Romaldkirk is a pretty Teesdale village formed by a number of stone-built houses surrounding a large and quite open village green. It is the first bridging point for motor traffic upstream of Barnard Castle. St Romald's Church is unusually large for such a small place and is nicknamed the 'cathedral of the dale' in consequence.

Romaldkirk is next to the B6277, which links Middleton in Teesdale to the larger market town of Barnard Castle, 6 miles away. The walk follows a section of the Teesdale Way down to and along the high banks of the Tees as far as Cotherstone village, returning across the fields. It links up with Walk 21 in Cotherstone village, so the two can be combined.

Starting Point:	The Rose and Crown Inn (Grid ref. NY 995221)
Distance:	4 or 5 miles
Terrain:	Mostly unsurfaced field and woodland paths.
Map:	OS Outdoor Leisure 31 Teesdale
Toilets:	Romaldkirk
Refreshments:	Rose and Crown Inn or Kirk Inn, Romaldkirk
Pushchairs:	Aside from the lanes around Romaldkirk village, this is not a recommended route for pushchairs.

☞ You should pass most of these. See how many you can spot:

☐ a cathedral that isn't

☐ a beech tree

☐ rapids

☐ a Teesdale Way sign

☐ a lattice bridge

☐ a holly bush

☐ an old railway viaduct

☐ a black-faced sheep

☐ a house called Hard Ings

☐ a red and a green gate

1. Start by facing the Rose and Crown. Head right, past the Kirk Inn and on to the village green.

☺ The green here is quite big – so is the church. In fact, that is so big that its nickname is the 'cathedral of the dale'.

2. Walk along in front of the Kirk Inn and join the waymarked public footpath straight ahead. Use this to leave the green between the stone cottages. Keep going to a waymarked gate. Pass through into a pasture.

Q: What species of tree are these?
A: Beech

3. Walk straight ahead to the last beech tree and then bear left to the top of the field's central mound. From here a single waymarked gate is visible. Walk down and through it to diagonally cross the next field. Pass through another gate and then head downhill towards a farmstead.

☺ The buildings ahead of us are Low Garth. The banks of the River Tees are just beyond.

4. At Low Garth, cross the stile beside the metal gate and turn left across the front of the farmhouse. Follow the grass path as it skirts the edge of the field to a waymarked stile in the bottom corner. Cross into the woods.

☺ Look down to the Tees on our left. We should be able to see some rapids.

5. Walk on. Cross the next stile and the stream immediately beyond it. Continue until you walk across a flat piece of ground on the inside of a river meander. Here a lane develops. Walk up to cross the stile at the top and then to pass through the succeeding gate before following the fence on your left that leads you on to the next habitation.

☺ The set of buildings we are now approaching is called Woden Croft.

6. At Woden Croft, pass along the lane to the left of the barn, through two gates, and then along the front of a row of cottages to a white metal gate. Pass through.

This section overlaps with Walk 21.

7. **Route A** is to the right – after passing through the gate. At the corner of the pasture a waymark arrow will direct you through a farm gate into some woods. Cross the beck, ignoring the isolated footbridge, and walk up the other side to the next gate. Pass through and carry straight on along the field edge until you cross a waymarked stone stile into the grounds of Thwaite Hall. Walk along the drive to the road.

Escape route: Turn right and walk along the road to Romaldkirk (about 1½ miles).

8. Turn left to walk as far as the bridge to Cotherstone village (the Balder Bridge). Turn right just before the road crosses the bridge.

Routes A and B join again here – see directions below from Balder Bridge.

9. To follow **Route B**, from the white gate, follow the Teesdale Way, which is straight ahead. A short lane leads you to a five-bar gate next to a stone building. Pass through and make your way down the pasture. As you descend you will see, at the bottom, two tree-surmounted hummocks. Walk between these, down to the still lower ground. Head right, and cross the stile you encounter. Drop down to cross the five stepping stones over a small tributary, and walk along with the fence on your right. Cross the next stile.

Q: What is not allowed along here?
A: A sign indicates that fishing is not allowed.

10. Follow the line of the fence to your left until you cross a further stile into the woods. Follow the path until you reach the end of the main footbridge, which crosses the Tees itself. Do not cross this, but continue straight ahead along the Teesdale Way until you cross a smaller bridge over a tributary.

☺ At this end of the bridge is Hunderthwaite. See if you can discover the name of the parish on the other side.

It is Cotherstone. This is written on the toadstool-shaped post at the other end of the bridge. The mound ahead of you is where Cotherstone Castle was built with a commanding view over this stretch of the Tees. You could climb the mound to explore the remains.

11. Turn right up the lane to Cotherstone village and then right, alongside the main road. Walk down towards the Balder Bridge.

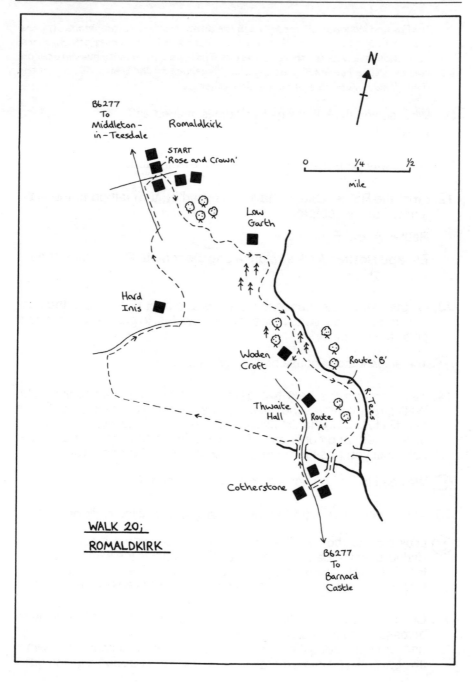

N

B6277
To
Middleton-
in-Teesdale

Romaldkirk

START
'Rose and Crown'

Low
Garth

Hard
Inis

Woden
Croft

Route 'B'

R. Tees

Thwaite
Hall

Route
'A'

Cotherstone

WALK 20;
ROMALDKIRK

B6277
To
Barnard
Castle

0   ¼   ½

mile

The Fox and Hounds pub opposite may be an appropriate refreshment stop. As pubs go, it is a little up-market. There is another pub and a post office general store along the village street to the left. The road can be quite busy in season, so care will be needed. On leaving the village, one of the last buildings on the right (Balder View) has an unusual weather vane.

Q: What do you think that weather vane is shaped as?

A: A fox.

Q: Which way does it show the wind to be blowing today?

12. From the Balder Bridge (having crossed it), turn left on to the way-marked public footpath.

Routes A and B join here.

Escape Route: Walk straight along the road to Romaldkirk (about 1½ miles).

13. On the main route, descend the steps and bear right across the pasture and up a rise to the fence line. Follow this, to pass through a gate on to a gravelly lane.

☺ The elegant stone house on the right is Dow Park.

14. Pass through the next two gates and cross the succeeding stile. Walk straight across the field and pass through the next gate. Cross the stile following that. However, ignore a further stile you may notice on your left, and continue to follow the fence round the edge of the field until you pass through a gap at the end of a hedgerow.

☺ We need to look out for a gate on the left along here.

15. At the gate, bear right to cross a waymarked stile. Walk on.

☺ Look over to the left. The bridge we can see is the disused railway viaduct over the Balder valley. The River Balder is the same tributary of the Tees which we crossed twice earlier – just before and after Cotherstone village. We will be crossing a disused railway cutting soon.

16. Cross the pair of ladder stiles, either side of the cutting, to walk across the pasture beyond to a red, metal farm gate. Pass through and turn right along the stony track. Follow this, rounding a rightward sweep, until you join a metalled lane, and then through a green gate.

Turn right on to the lane and walk along until you come to a house on the left.

☺ This house is called Hard Ings.

17. Turn left on to the track beside the house. Cross the next stile to a lane that brings you through a gap in the hedgerow, and eventually to a gate. Pass through, past a small, stone store, and down to the field corner. Turn left and walk up to the stile on your right. Cross it and walk to the crest of the field. From here, walk ahead to a gate and beyond that, cut the corner of the next pasture to another gate. Pass through and walk over to the concrete barn on your left. Follow the painted arrows to pass the house there and walk down the lane to the road. Turn left and walk back to Romaldkirk.

The Rose and Crown, Romaldkirk

Other Places of Interest in the Area

Barnard Castle, Middleton in Teesdale, Low and High Force

For all of these, see Walk 18.

21. COTHERSTONE

Cotherstone is a village in Teesdale. It is a linear village, situated on the B6277, some 3½ miles west of Barnard Castle. Perhaps its principal claim to fame is soft Cotherstone cheese – a slightly tangy cow's cheese and a personal favourite of mine. Try some! Some bar meals in the Fox and Hounds incorporate it as an ingredient, and you may find it for sale in Middleton or Barnard Castle.

The walk begins and ends in the village itself, and takes in a most attractive section of the Teesdale Way along the wooded banks of the upper Tees. The steep descent from the castle mound offers a splendid view over the river, enhanced by the elegant, green-latticed Victorian footbridge.

Starting Point: Cotherstone village, Red Lion pub (Grid ref. NZ 012197)

Distance: 2½ miles

Terrain: Most of the walk is on unsurfaced field and woodland paths. There are no especially steep ascents on these, though the stepped descent from the castle mound does have a steep gradient. Part of the latter, return leg, is on metalled road.

Map: OS Outdoor Leisure 31 Teesdale

Toilets: Red Lion and Fox and Hounds pubs in Cotherstone village.

Refreshments: Red Lion and Fox and Hounds pubs in Cotherstone village, and Cotherstone village shop.

Pushchairs: Apart from the village itself, and the early part of Demesne Lane, this is not a pushchair walk.

☞ You should pass most of these. See how many you can spot:

☐   a school
☐   a drystone wall
☐   allotments
☐   ponies
☐   holly
☐   a black-faced sheep
☐   a cattle grid
☐   a goat
☐   a wooden barn
☐   a blue caravan

The Tees at Cotherstone

1. Start as though you were coming out of the front door of the Red Lion. Cross the road and head right until you are opposite the school. The road begins to bend right. Take the lane on your left.

Q: What is the name of the house on the right?

A: Featherstone House

2. Reach the waymark post after Featherstone House but ignore it and follow the lane round to the right to pass a house with birdcages in the garden. Continue along Demesne Lane, passing the entrance road for the mill on the left, and carrying straight ahead until the stony lane turns left across a cattle grid. Follow the lane round to the left.

☺ Cattle grids work for sheep, too. The idea is that animals cannot walk over the bars, so the grid stops them straying out of their fields without the need for a gate – which can be a nuisance to have to open and close all the time and which careless people might leave open. When we are walking in the country we must always close the gates we do meet so that animals can be kept safely in their fields.

Q: You can see Cotherstone church over to the left. What is special about its design?

A: Unusually for this area, it has a spire rather than a tower.

If you have the OS map with you, you may like to show the children the different symbols for churches with (and without) towers and spires, and maybe look for examples of each in and around Teesdale.

3. The lane brings you to a crash barrier above the steep river cliff. Turn left on to the grassy path, which runs along the top of the cliff. Walk along to, and through, a waymarked single wooden gate.

☺ The river at the bottom of the cliff is the Tees. You can see boulders strewn across the river's course. When the river is full, after heavy rain or snow has melted, for instance, it can pick up these large stones and carry them downstream.

4. Keep going and pass through the narrow, stone gap stile you reach, adjacent to a five-bar gate. Cross the farm track which sweeps down to the right, and carry straight on along the cliff top path until you pass a farmstead below you on the right.

Ahead is a railing-enclosed grave. Depending how you feel about this, you may suggest the children go on ahead to find out about it. The plaque is to the mem-

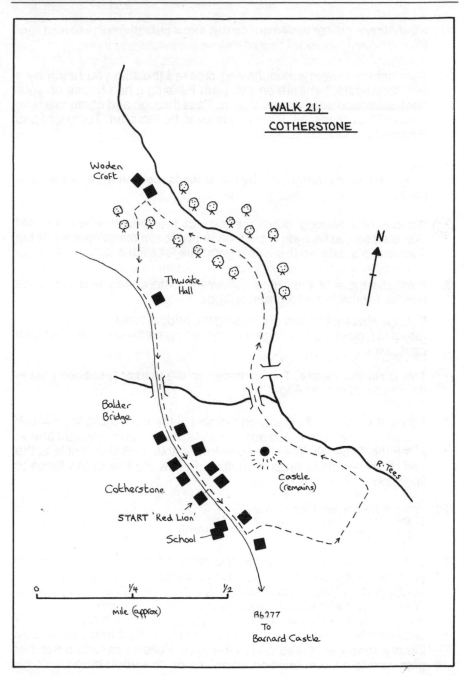

WALK 21;
COTHERSTONE

Woden Croft

Thwaite Hall

N

Balder Bridge

R. Tees

Cotherstone

Castle (remains)

START 'Red Lion'

School

0　　　　¼　　　　½

mile (approx)

Bb277
To
Barnard Castle

ory of Abraham Hilton of Barnard Castle, a local philanthropist who died aged 87 in 1882 and was buried here at his own request.

5.   Turn right, as waymarked, having crossed the stile you reach by a red, metal gate, beneath an ash tree. Passing a hen house on your right, approach another metal gate. Pass through and come to a lane turning 90 degrees left. Do not, however, be tempted. Turn right and descend the footpath steps.

Q: How many steps are there?
A: 12 to start, then a further 27 (by the author's reckoning), and then a final 11.

☺ We are now walking down the side of the mound where the old Cotherstone Castle was. It must have had a commanding view of the Tees and the dale, so this was a good site for such a fort.

6.   From the base of the steps, follow the path ahead and cross the smaller footbridge with green railings.

Escape Route: Instead of crossing the bridge, turn left up the lane to return to Cotherstone village, turning left again to reach the Red Lion start point.

☺ This is Hunderthwaite. This is written on the toadstool-shaped post at the other end of the bridge.

7.   Follow the path until you reach the end of the main footbridge which crosses the Tees itself. Do not cross this, but continue straight ahead along the Teesdale Way. Keep following this, crossing a stile at the end of the woods to enter a pasture. Follow the line of the fence to your right.

Q: What is not allowed along here?
A: A sign indicates that fishing is not allowed.

8.   Cross the stile you encounter and carry on with the fence now on your left. Keep going until you have crossed five stepping stones over a small tributary. Walk up the rise to cross a stile into a pasture. Walk straight ahead, but keeping to the lower ground until you are level with the gap between two tree-surmounted hummocks to your left. Head left and through this gap. Then bear right and walk over to the drystone wall ahead and to the right. Follow this until a five-bar gate next to a stone building leads you on to a short lane.

Q: Which way does the Teesdale Way take us next?

A: Waymarking at the end of the short lane indicates the Teesdale Way is straight ahead.

9. Continue to the next gateway, to the left of a drystone walled garden. Reaching a pair of white gates, you will find waymarking in all directions. The route is to the left – not passing through either gate.

10. At the corner of the pasture a waymark arrow will direct you through a farm gate into some woods. Cross the beck, ignoring the isolated footbridge, and walk up the other side to the next gate. Pass through and carry straight on along the field edge until you cross a waymarked stone stile into the grounds of Thwaite Hall. Walk along the drive to the road and turn left to return to Cotherstone village.

The road can be quite busy in season, so care will be needed. On entering the village, one of the first buildings on the left (Balder View) has an unusual weather vane.

Q: What do you think that the weather vane is shaped as?

A: A fox.

Q: Which way does it show the wind to be blowing today?

Other Places of Interest in the Area

Barnard Castle, Middleton in Teesdale, Low and High Force

For all of these, see Walk 18.

22. MIDDLETON ONE ROW

The walk begins on the village green of this Georgian backwater village, leading you through woodlands by the Tees to the tiny but picturesque settlement of Low Dinsdale. It returns to Middleton via a slightly higher route, partly across a golf course, offering open views across to the Cleveland Hills.

The walk is quite easy, without steep ascents, though the woodland paths may become muddy during and following wet weather. The green at Middleton One Row has seats and would make a good picnic spot, as well as affording plentiful runabout space for children. The window and outdoor seats of the Davenport pub offer views of both the Tees Valley and playing children.

Starting Point:	The Davenport, Middleton One Row (Grid ref. NZ 353123)
Distance:	4 miles
Terrain:	The first half of the walk is mostly on unsurfaced woodland paths. The return leg is a combination of field paths and lanes, some surfaced. There are no steep climbs.
Map:	OS Pathfinder 600 Darlington
Public Toilets:	Middleton One Row village green
Refreshments:	Middleton One Row
Pushchairs:	The village itself and much of the second half of the walk are suitable for pushchairs, though you may have to lift over the odd stile.

☞ You should pass most of these. See how many you can spot:

☐ a Teesdale Way sign

☐ an ash tree

☐ rosehips

☐ someone fishing

☐ ponies

☐ an aircraft

☐ holly

☐ a grain hopper

☐ hay bales

☐ ducks on a pond

1. Start as though walking out of the front door of the Davenport Hotel, crossing the road to the village green. Walk to the right and then diagonally left across the green, passing the parish council signboard on your way down to the corner of the woods.

2. Enter the woods beside a large ash tree.

Q: How many steps are there to walk down?
A: 13.

3. Along the river bank you will come across some half moon-shaped constructions in the slope on your left, edged with a kind of wooden palisade. You might ask the children to say what they think these are for. They are to protect the river bank form erosion by the river, especially after heavy rain when there will be a lot of water flowing quickly through the channel.

4. Keep following the wooded riverside path, crossing a footbridge along the way, until you reach a waymarked stile at the entrance to some private grounds.

Q: Which cottage do the gates allow access to?
A: Bath Cottage

5. Follow the Teesdale Way left into the grounds and keep to the path along the riverbank.

Beside the large house with balconies (Dinsdale Spa) there is an alternative route along the lower drive, which is waymarked, and which you may prefer in wet weather.

Q: Which fishing club has a notice along here and what does it say?
A: Darlington Brown Trout Association. Fishing upstream is strictly private.

6. Keep going along the path as it rises after a footbridge crossing and then descends into a glade crossed by a brick-built bridge. Cross the bridge and continue until there is a T-junction of paths. Bear left.

☺ Looking left through the trees you may be able to catch glimpses of Middleton One Row. If you are lucky enough to hear church bells chiming, these will be from the church at Low Dinsdale, which you are nearing.

7. At the edge of the wood, cross the stile and walk on over the sheep pasture ahead in the direction of the telegraph pole. Then bear left towards the church. Pass through the gate and turn right along the lane.

8. Have a look at the church tower.

Q: What time does the clock say?

Q: What is unusual about the tower?

A: The tower is built of red-coloured sandstone — a colour of stone not normally found in this region.

The postbox here is very old — probably about 100 years. The letters VR mean that it dates from the reign of Queen Victoria. What time is the next collection due?

☺ As you walk along the lane the first cottage has a date.

Q: When was that cottage built?

A: 1851.

On either side of the lane are hedgerows. In many parts of the countryside hedgerows have been removed in recent years. You could discuss this issue. Why have farmers removed hedges? (To allow more space to grow crops and for bigger machines, so yields and financial returns are greater.) Why do some people object? (Loss of habitat for animals and of plant species, reduced windbreak function accelerating soil erosion.)

9. Continue to follow the lane as it rounds a right-hand bend.

☺ The farmhouse on the right is the Manor House. You may already have noticed that there are slight bumps, referred to on the OS map as 'earthworks', in the adjacent field. These are the remains of a previous larger and fortified Norman manor house.

Low Dinsdale is a tiny remnant of an earlier larger medieval farming village. Clearance of such villages sometimes occurred in succeeding centuries as land was re-organised by estate owners. On other occasions, the process of enclosure, by which the large, open fields of the Middle Ages were converted into the hedged patchwork of medium-sized fields often associated with the English countryside, led to the loss or shrinking of old agricultural villages. The Black Death in the 14th century had the same effect.

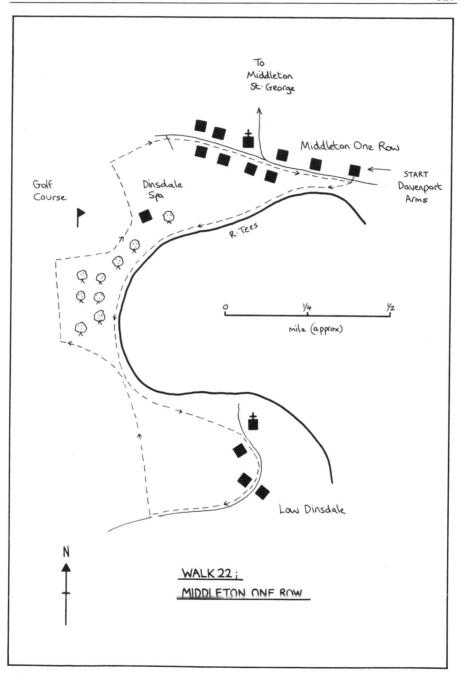

To
Middleton
St. George

Middleton One Row

START
Davenport
Arms

Golf
Course

Dinsdale
Spa

R. Tees

0   ¼   ½

mile (approx)

Low Dinsdale

N

WALK 22 ;

MIDDLETON ONE ROW

10. Ignoring the Teesdale Way marker on your left, keep walking along the lane until you have rounded a further rightward kink in the road. Turn right through a waymarked metal gate by an ash tree on to a field path. Walk straight ahead along the edge of the field, ignoring a waymarked stile on your right.

☺ The hills you can see over to the right are the Cleveland Hills. They are the start of the North Yorkshire Moors. Looking further round to the left you can see Middleton One Row again.

11. Keep walking along the track as the hedge on your right becomes the edge of a wood, and don't be tempted to turn down into the wood.

Q: What crop is growing in the field?

12. Suddenly you will come upon a golf tee on your left. Simply continue straight ahead.

☺ A golf tee is where golfers begin to hit the ball for each hole on a golf course. This part of the walk is going to take us across some of the Middleton St George Golf Course. It is a public right of way though, so we are allowed to walk along the path. On the tee, the sign tells golfers which hole this is, how long it is and how many shots it should take.

Q: What does the sign say about this hole?
A: It is the 7th hole, 328 metres long, and a par 4.

13. Carry on along the path, rounding the right-hand bend and crossing another section of golf course.

Q: Which number hole is shown by the flag here?
A: 4.

☺ There are bunkers here. These are part of the game of golf and are traps which players try to avoid, so they don't end up losing shots.

Look out for the warning sign ahead, 'Beware golf balls off 18th tee before approaching 18th green.'

14. Leave the golf course and turn right down the lane. Follow the lane around a left-hand bend, ignoring a gate on the right.

Q: What is the building ahead used for?

Middleton One Row

15. Keep walking along the lane until you reach a waymarked stile on your left. Cross this on to another section of golf course. Follow the public footpath ahead between the 9th green and a group of trees. Pass the pond on your left and make for the seat ahead.

Q: What type of tree are those by the seat?

A: Oak trees

16. Now make for the waymarked gap in the corner of the boundary ahead. Pass through it and turn right to walk along the path on the right-hand edge of the field.

Talk about the crop growing in the field, or, depending on season, what state the field is in (fallow, recently ploughed etc.).

17. Walk on until you emerge on a metalled road via a 5-bar gate.

☺ Looking to the left here you can see part of a Roman road. You can tell that because it is so straight.

You could talk about why the Romans built such straight roads (speed of movement, military purpose, no need to bother about property in the way) and later people have built roads with more bends (ease of movement, avoiding steep hills and other obstacles).

18. Walk straight ahead, not on to the Roman road, and follow the road back to Middleton One Row.

☺ There are two questions on the way back.

Q: What is unusual about a path we pass?

A: A turnstile at its end.

Q: Who is commemorated by the lych gate plaque?

A: Revd Jackson.

19. Keep going straight on to return to 'The Front' — the row in Middleton One Row.

Other Places of Interest in the Area

Teesside International Airport

Teesside Airport is no Heathrow, but it is close by. Follow the signs from Middleton St George. There is a viewing platform and aircraft movements of both light aircraft and some more substantial airliners to see.

Butterfly World in Preston Park

Preston Park is the grounds of a large, nineteenth-century house (Preston Hall) converted into a museum. It includes a recreated Victorian High Street, and is run by Stockton Borough Council (telephone 01642 393949 for the park and 781184 for Preston Hall Museum). In the park are children's play areas, crazy golf, aviaries and Butterfly World. This latter is a privately run attraction and there is a charge. Opening hours vary according to season (telephone 01642 791414 for details) and there is a period of winter closure. It is a large greenhouse housing tropical vegetation and many vividly coloured free-flying butterflies, as well as fish, which children can feed, in its watercourse. As a rainy day venue, it is excellent. Preston Park is well signposted and is off the A135, Yarm Road, Eaglescliffe.

Also of Interest

NORTHUMBERLAND TOWNS & VILLAGES
Lydia Speakman

The essential guide to this history-rich county - a comprehensive reference book containing a section on all the main settlements highlighting the key buildings, landscape and wildlife of the area, together with the stories and legends associated with each community. Perfect for visitors, and those interested in their local history. £7.95

BEST TEA SHOP WALKS IN NORTHUMBRIA
Stephen Rickerby

Good fresh northern air and a decent northern tea to follow! These 21, varied walks from the Tees to within 4 miles of the Scottish border, each begin and end at a tea shop of character and interest. The walks vary from 2 to a little over 5 miles in length and include careful directions (with a map) for a leisurely ramble in the open air. £6.95

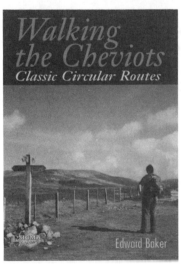

WALKING THE CHEVIOTS
Edward Baker

This is one of the few guides to a true wilderness area, written by an experienced author who has lived in the Cheviots all his life. Nearly 50 walks, from 2 to 14 miles. "This book is a must for the Cheviot walker, whether experienced in the area or a visitor eager to explore this unique range of northern hills" - RAMBLING TODAY. £7.95

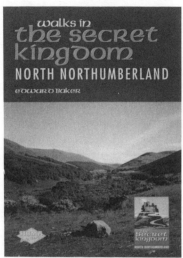

WALKS IN THE SECRET KINGDOM: North Northumberland
Edward Baker

Explore the varied landscape and unique character of the undiscovered kingdom of North Northumberland with this book of easy-to-follow, flexible routes. "This book will appeal to all ages, from the long-distance walk hunter, to the family group just wanting to fill in a few hours... and at the same time get some worthwhile exercise." BORDER TELEGRAPH. £6.95

BEST PUB WALKS ON TYNESIDE
Lydia Speakman & Richard Baker

With this book, Tyneside - already an area noted for its quality beer and pubs - will become renowned for its fine walking. £6.95

POETRY IN THE PARKS: a celebration of the national parks of England and Wales
Wendy Bardsley

A celebration of the 50th anniversary of the National Parks in poetry and photographs, including specially commissioned verse by some of the outstanding poets of this generation. Poems spanning centuries reflect the landscape's enduring power to inspire, accompanied by superb photographs. £9.95

LYDIA SPEAKMAN & RICHARD BAKER

Our books are available through all booksellers. In case of difficulty, or for a free catalogue, please contact: SIGMA LEISURE, 1 SOUTH OAK LANE, WILMSLOW, CHESHIRE SK9 6AR.
Phone: 01625-531035 Fax: 01625-536800. E-mail: info@sigmapress.co.uk
Web site: http//www.sigmapress.co.uk
MASTERCARD and VISA orders welcome.